Xanpan

Team Centric Agile Software
Development

Allan Kelly

Xanpan
Team Centric Agile Software Development

Allan Kelly

This book is for sale at http://www.xanpan.org

This version was published on 2014-04-26

This is a Leanpub book. Leanpub empowers authors and publishers with the Lean Publishing process. Lean Publishing is the act of publishing an in-progress ebook using lightweight tools and many iterations to get reader feedback, pivot until you have the right book and build traction once you do.

Contents

Twitter & other online media

Please Tweet!

Please help Allan Kelly spread the word about this book on Twitter.

Allan's Twitter handle is @allankellynet, and the hashtag for this book and all things Xanpan is #xanpan.

Find out what others are saying about this book on Twitter with this link:

> http://twitter.com/search/#xanpan

Websites

There are two websites to accompany this book. The first is the LeanPub page and the second the author's own:

> http://leanpub.com/xanpan
>
> http://www.xanpan.org

And the author's own website is:

> http://www.allankelly.net

What people say about Xanpan....

"Allan Kelly's Xanpan is now required reading for our team"

Dom Davis Head of IT, Virgin Wines.

"A well written and insightful reference material, packs a punch throughout!!!"

Sunish Chabba

"Finished @allankellynet 's book XanPan http://nud.gr/1fNSSxF if you're doing agile, lean, Kanban, xp a mix of any or just starting read it"

Kev McCabe @BigMadKev on Twitter

If you have something nice to say about this book please consider submitting a quote to add to this page. Please e-mail xanpan@allankelly.net with your quote, name and position and if we we like it we'll add it in a future edition.

About the author

Allan Kelly has held just about every job in IT. London-based, he works for Software Strategy, where he provides training and consultancy in Agile practices. He specialises in working with software product companies, aligning company strategy with products and processes.

He wrote his first program at the age of 12 on a Sinclair ZX81, in Basic. He quickly progressed beyond the ZX81 and spent the mid-80's programming the BBC Micro in BBC Basic, 6502 Assembler, Pascal and Forth. As well as appearing in several hobbyist magazines of the time, he was a regular on BBC Telesoftware, with programs such as Printer Dump Program (PDP and PDR), Eclipse, Snapshot, Echos, Fonts, FEMCOMS and, with David Halligan, Demon's Tomb, and EMACS (Envelop Manipulation and Control System, nothing to do with its more famous namesake!).

The low point of this early career came in 1986 when Cambridge Examinations docked a mark from his GCE 'O' level Computer Science project for not using the GOTO statement in his code. The high point came five years later when he held an internship at Distributed Information Processing in Guildford, working on the Sharp PC-3000.

He believes his first Agile project was in 1997 - although it might have been 1994. His Agile journey began after the Railtrack Aplan ISO-Waterfall death march in 1996 and reading Jim Mc-Carthy's Dynamics of Software Development (1995). Since 2000 he has helped numerous companies - particularly in Cornwall - adopt Agile and Lean ideas.

In addition to numerous journal articles and conference presentations, he is the author of *Business Patterns for Software Developers* (2012) and *Changing Software Development: Learning to be Agile* (2008), both published by John Wiley & Sons. He is also the originator of Retrospective Dialogue Sheets (www.dialoguesheets.com).

More about Allan at http://www.allankelly.net and on Twitter as @allankellynet[1].

---

[1]https://twitter.com/allankellynet

Introduction

Is it possible to write a book by accident? Maybe not, but I certainly seem to have started writing one by accident.

This book is several things: first it captures my personal experience, understanding and reflections on the thing we call 'Agile'. Second, it describes a type of Agile working - an Agile method if you like - I call *Xanpan*. Xanpan is itself the result of my experience, understanding and reflections.

The world doesn't need another Agile method, or indeed any other software development method for that matter. The real point of Xanpan is not that it is a development method. Rather, the significance of Xanpan is that it is a derived method, it is a hybrid method, it is an example of a method that anyone could create.

Xanpan is both a method and a philosophy - my philosophy on how software is, or should be, created, and how Agile works - or should work. While I have every reason to believe it is applicable in fields beside software development I have not had a chance to try it to date.

As the name suggests, it is a cross between Extreme Programming (XP) (Beck 2000) and Kanban (Anderson 2010). It is also an elaboration of the process first described as Blue-White-Red (Kelly 2007), which was itself an implementation of XP ideas. Xanpan also contains ideas, techniques and approaches from other methods and schools of thought, specifically product management.

Like all Agile processes, Xanpan rests on Lean thinking (Womack and Jones 2005; Womack, Jones, and Roos 1991; M. Poppendieck and Poppendieck 2003) for its underlying philosophy and principles. As such it may be described as 'Agile' or 'Lean'.

At first sight Xanpan probably does not look vastly different from XP or Scrum. But by making several tweaks to the iteration the process flow is enhanced and emphasised: work can be carried between iterations, teams are not asked to commit personally and unplanned work is allowed for.

I think the best way to discuss Xanpan is to step through an example and point out where it differs from other methods - specifically Scrum and Kanban. So after a brief look at some principles behind Xanpan, the description moves to examples, interspersed with explanation and notes on practice.

Xanpan originates in software development, and the description here assumes it is used in a software development area. However it is expected that Xanpan, with modifications, may be used in other domains. At the time of writing there are too few examples to support a description of uses outside software.

More importantly, Xanpan demonstrates how ideas from Agile, Lean and elsewhere, brought together with one's own experiences, can be the basis for a coherent method. Exploring the roots, principles and laws behind Xanpan thinking fulfils two roles: firstly it exposes what I consider to be the logic of software development, and secondly it shows how to build an approach with depth.

Xanpan wasn't born fully formed, it wasn't built bottom up from principles; while practice drove development top-down, there is a back story - there are principles which informed the development. Only when - if - this book is complete might Xanpan be considered anything near fully formed. Even then it will continue to grow and evolve.

I have long advocated that teams need to 'roll their own' development methods - this was a minor theme in *Changing Software Development* (Kelly 2008). Look at Scrum, yes steal from XP, certainly learn about Kanban and let it permeate your working. But above all, combine the parts of methods that work for you.

All development methods seem to say 'tailor this method to your own needs'. The difference between traditional - including SSADM, PRINCE 2, RUP and others - and Agile methods - Scrum, XP, Kanban, etc. - is that the former start large and say 'Tailor this method down', while the latter start small and say (if only implicitly) 'Tailor this method up'.

Indeed, Agile methods have been called 'barely sufficient' - they lack a lot of the details and contingency tools present in other methods. This makes them easy to tailor, but also makes tailoring essential.

Xanpan is an example of how I have rolled these ideas together and helped many teams adopt a similar style of working tailored to their own needs. A later chapter discusses the origins of Xanpan in more depth.

Depending on your point of view, Xanpan is a tailored version of Extreme Programming, or a tailored version of Kanban. The context of Xanpan tailoring is:

- Teams initially adopting Agile development
- Organisations that have generally stable teams
- Software development groups in Europe, and in particular the United Kingdom

I hope this book still offers useful content to those outside this context, but I can't guarantee it!

After saying all that, if changing the world does require another methodology, I am more than happy to offer Xanpan, and would be delighted to hear of more teams adopting Xanpan.

Why write another book about Agile?

There is no shortage of books about Agile available today, and specifically Agile software development. So why write another one?

Three reasons really, three reasons that also happen to define the audience - or is it the three audiences that define the reason?

- The Experienced: think of this book as a post-Scrum book. The world needed XP and Scrum when they appeared in the late 1990s. Many teams have really benefitted from simply 'doing Scrum by the book'. But the world has moved on, we have all learned.

  This book captures one person's learning, the author's, and encourages teams to use their own experience and learning to create post-Scrum methods that work for them.

- The Newcomers: when asked "What book would you recommend for newcomers?", I'm never quite sure what to answer. In part this book answers that question - and conveniently gives the author something to give to students attending his introductory Agile training courses.
- The Author: as all authors discover, writing forces one to clarify one's ideas, put them in a communicative form and in doing so deepen one's understanding. When I first started using the term 'Xanpan' I didn't know what I was getting into. The more I used it, the more people wanted to know and the more I realised there was to it. This manuscript allows me to put my thinking into a coherent whole.

Conscience drives the author to apologise for writing for himself. But he does not. Writing a book, even compiling and editing existing material, is a long and lonely process. *Business Patterns for Software Developers* was to be the last book - at least for a while. Instead the author finds himself at work on another book.

This and subsequent books

At the moment this book is a detailed account of the Xanpan process. In my mind this is but one part of three - should I ever write them. One additional volume will look at requirements and another at the management of software development. Initially these will appear as individual volumes and later as one complete book, possibly.

Astute readers of this book through its various incarnations on

LeanPub will notice a change in the title of this book. The early versions which appeared in 2013 were titled:

Xanpan: Personal reflections on Agile & Software Development

This book still summarises my personal reflections, or sense-making if you prefer, on Agile-type software development. However starting with the 2014 editions the title has been updated to:

Xanpan: Team Centric Agile Software Development

This reflects repeated observation from those who have read this book or seen my presentations on Xanpan. It is the team, not the project or product, which is the heart of Xanpan. This marks it out as subtlety different from other methods and I think more accurately reflects my own thinking on Agile development. Should I ever complete the management volume of Xanpan this aspect should be even clearer.

Saying Xanpan is *team centric* also helps reconcile a conflict within Xanpan. On the one hand Xanpan is a process a team could pick up and use. On the other hand Xanpan aims to say "create your own process, don't follow someone else's prescription."

If the essence of Xanpan is the team then any team which step-up and actively create and agree their own process can be said to be following Xanpan.

Feedback

Although I increasing think this book is finished I continue to think of things I should, or could, change, or add. The nature of LeanPub books raises a question of: when is a book finished?

For the moment I think this book is mostly done. However as the later volumes are written there are bound to be changes to this one.

I would also like to encourage readers to send me their comments about the book and suggestions for improvement. Please send e-mail to **xanpan@allankelly.net**.

Coupons & freebies

Finally, as I produce new versions of this book and subsequent volumes I may decide to add some discounts and coupons for existing readers. I will place these at the very back of the book. Please check the last few pages of the book.

References

Anderson, D. 2010. *Kanban.* Blue Hole Press.

Beck, K. 2000. *Extreme Programming Explained.* Addison-Wesley.

Kelly, A. 2007. "Blue White Red - an example agile process." *ACCU Overload* (81).

———. 2008. *Changing Software Development: Learning to Become Agile.* John Wiley & Sons.

Poppendieck, M., and T. Poppendieck. 2003. *Lean Software Development. Agile Software Development Series.* Addison-Wesley.

Womack, J. P., D. T. Jones, and D. Roos. 1991. *The machine that changed the world.* New York: HaperCollins.

Womack, J. P., and D. T. Jones. 2005. *Lean Solutions.* London: Simon & Schuster.

Prologue

Dear Customer: The Truth About IT Projects

Dear customer,

I think it's time we in the IT industry came clean about how we charge you, why our bills are sometimes a bit higher than you might expect, and why so many IT projects result in disappointment. The truth is that when we start an IT project, we don't know how much time and effort it will take to complete. Consequently, we don't know how much it will cost. This may not be a message you want to hear, particularly since you are absolutely certain you know what you want.

Herein lies another truth, which I'll try to put as politely as I can. You are, after all, a customer, and, really, I shouldn't offend you. You know the saying "The customer is always right"? The thing is, you don't know what you want. You may know in general terms, but the devil is in the detail - and the more detail you try to give us beforehand, the more likely your desires are to change. Each time you give us more detail, you are offering more hostages to fortune.

Software engineering expert Capers Jones believes the things you want ('requirements', as we like to call them) change 2% per month on average - thats close to 27% over a year once you compound changes. Personally, I'm surprised that number is so low.

Just to complicate matters, the world is uncertain. Things change, and companies go out of business. Remember Enron? Remember Lehman Brothers? Customer tastes change. Remember Cabbage Patch Kids? Fashion changes, governments change, and competitors do their best to make life hard. So, really, even if you do know absolutely what you want when you first speak to us, it is unlikely that it will stay the same for very long.

I'm afraid to say that there are people in the IT industry who will take advantage of this situation. They will smile and agree with you when you tell them what you want, right up to the point when you sign. From then on, it's a different story; they know that changes are inevitable, and they plan to make a healthy profit from change requests and late additions at your expense.

While I'm being honest, it is true we sometimes gold-plate things. You might not need a data warehouse for your online retailer on day one. Yes, some of our engineers like to do more than what is needed, and yes, we have a vested interest in getting things added so that we can charge you more.

It is also true that you quite legitimately think of features and functionality you would like after we've begun. You naturally assume something is 'in' when we assume it is 'out'. And, in the spirit of openness, can you honestly say that you've never tried to put one over on us? (Let's not even talk about bugs right now: it just complicates everything.)

Frankly, given all this, it is touching that you have so much faith in technology to deliver. But when IT does deliver, does it deliver big. Look what it did for Bill Gates and Larry Page, or Amazon and FedEx. Isn't it interesting that when the IT industry develops things for itself, we end up with multi-millionaires? When we develop for other people, they end up losing money.

How did we ever talk you into any of this? Well, we package this unsightly mess and try to sell it to you. To do this, we have to hide all this unpleasantness. We start with a ritual called 'estimation' - how much time we think the work will take. These 'estimates' are little better than guesses. Humans can't estimate time. We've known this since at least the late '70s, when Kahneman and Tversky described the 'planning fallacy' in 1979 and went on to win a Nobel Prize. Basically, humans consistently underestimate how long work will take and are overconfident in their estimates.

To make things worse, we have a bad habit we really should kick. Between estimating the work and doing the work, we usually change the team. The estimate may be made by the IT equivalent of Manchester United or the New York Yankees, but the team that actually does the work is more than likely a rag-tag bunch of coders, analysts and managers who've never met before.

Historical data - data about estimates, actuals, costs, etc - can help inform planning, but most companies don't have their own data. For those that do have data, most of it is worse than useless. In fact, Capers Jones suggests that inaccurate historical data is a major cause of project failure. For example, software engineers rarely get paid overtime, so tracking systems often miss these extra hours. Indeed, some companies prohibit employees from logging more than their official hours in their systems.

So we make this guess (sorry, 'estimate') and double it - or we might even triple it. If the new number looks too high, we might reduce it. Once our engineers have finished massaging the number, we give it to the sales folk, who massage it some more. After all, we want you to say "yes" to the biggest sticker price we can get. That might sound awful, but remember: we could have guessed higher in the first place.

Please don't shoot me: I'm only the messenger.

We don't know which number is 'right', but to make it acceptable to you, we pretend it is certain and we take on the risk. We can only do this if the number is sufficiently padded (and, even then, we go wrong). If the risk pays off, we get a fat profit. If it doesn't, we don't get any profit and may take a loss. If it's really bad, you don't get anything and we end up in Court or bust.

The alternative is that you take on the risk - and the mess - and do it yourself. Unfortunately, another sad truth is that in-house IT is generally even worse than that provided by specialists. For a software company development is a core competency - such companies live or die by their ability to deliver software, and if they are bad, they cease to trade. Evolution weeds out the poor performers. Corporate IT on the other hand rarely destroys a business - although it may damage profits. Indeed, Capers Jones' research also suggests specialist providers are generally better than corporate IT departments.

Sales folk might be absent, but the whole estimation process is open to gaming from many other sources and for many other reasons. The bottom line: if you decide to take on the risk, you may actually increase risk.

I know this sounds like a no-win scenario. You could just sit on the fence and wait for Microsoft or Google to solve your problems with a packaged solution, but will your competitors stand still while you do? Will you still be running a business when Google produces a free version?

Beware snake oil salesmen selling off-the-shelf applications. Once people start talking about 'customisation' or 'configuration', you head down a slippery slope. Configuring a large SAP installation is not a matter of selecting Tools, Options and then ticking a box. Configuring large packages is a major software development activity, no matter what you have been told. The people who undertake the configuration might be called 'consultants', but they are really specialist software developers, programmers by another name.

There really isn't a nice, simple solution to any of this. We can't solve this problem for you. We need you, but you have to work with us. As the customer, you have to be prepared to work with us, the supplier, again and again in order to reduce the risk. Addressing risks in a timely and cost-effective manner involves business-level decisions and trade-offs. If you aren't there to help, we can either make the decision for you (adding the risk that you disagree), or spend your time and money to address it.

You need to be prepared to accept and share the risk with us. If you aren't prepared to take on any risk, we will charge you a lot for all the risk we take on. Sharing the risk has the effect of reducing the risk, because once the risk is shared you, the customer, are motivated to reduce risk. One of the major risks on IT projects is a lack of customer involvement. You can help with that just by staying involved.

Ultimately all risk is your risk: you are the customer, you are paying for the project one way or another. If it fails to deliver value, it is your business that will suffer. When you share risks, when you are involved closely, risks can be addressed immediately rather than being allowed to fester and grow.

Finally, you may have grand ambitious, but we need to work in small chunks. I know this may not sound very sexy, but software creation works best when small. Economies of scale don't exist. In fact, we have diseconomies of scale, so we need to work in tiny pieces again, again and again. If you are prepared to accept these suggestions, then let's press 'reset' on our relationship and talk some more.

Yours sincerely,

The IT Industry

Originally published in the now defunct Agile Journal, March 2012

1 Xanpan Principles

Boiling Xanpan down to a core results in a few principles that guide thinking, and lead to a number of specific practices. Most of these principles and practices will look familiar to anyone who has worked with Agile and studied Scrum, Kanban or XP. However, Xanpan's formulation is subtly different from all of these: it mixes these principles and practices differently.

Deeper still, underlying all of these are even deeper principles and laws. Some of these are specific to the software industry - I will elaborate these later - and some are broader still. The key, deepest, principles I refer to as 'Philosophy'. These make up the "I think therefore I am" bedrock.

1.1 Work in iterations

The iteration, or sprint, is a well-established Agile practice. Working in regular cycles provides a rhythm to work, and also imposes a deadline - actually, a recurring deadline. As I have discussed elsewhere, humans are actually quite good at working to deadlines. Xanpan seeks to harness this effect by having teams work in fixed length iterations.

I like to use the train metaphor. A traditional project is like a train leaving London King's Cross for Edinburgh Waverley station. Trains are infrequent, about every two hours if memory serves. And to get the cheapest tickets, you need to book in advance. As a result we check the timetable in advance, we book our ticket, and if there is any doubt about who needs to go on the train, or what we need to take, we take it. The risk of leaving something behind is too high.

I arrive at the station in plenty of time. If while I'm waiting a colleague phones and says "Hey, we're having a beer in the Euston Flyer - want to join us for a quick half?", then I look at my watch and say "Sorry, my train leaves in 15 minutes". The risk to my schedule is too high, so I avoid changes. In the extreme, if one of my colleagues is late arriving for the train, I try to hold it back, I argue with the guard, I beg, I hold the door open in the hope my colleague makes the train.

When the train does leave I immediately call Edinburgh to say "I'm on my way"; when the train becomes late, I deny it or hope it will fix itself. Then I think "Well the taxi at the other end will only take 5 minutes, not the 20 I allowed". Eventually the whole train is late; with other passengers, I argue with the guard to throw some people and packages off the train to make it go faster.

Eventually the train calls at Edinburgh Haymarket, and everyone gets off saying "That's close enough".

In contrast, working in iterations is the equivalent of getting the London Underground. It isn't perfect, it has problems, but generally trains run, and they run regularly. I enter the Underground when I am ready; except for the first and last trains of the day, nobody checks the timetable.

If a train pulls in and it is over-crowded, I can decide: squeeze onto a packed train, or wait two minutes for the next. If I am lucky there is a sign that tells me how many minutes the next one will be. And if while I'm waiting someone calls me and says

"We are in the St Pancras Champagne Bar, fancy a drink?" I have an option. I can decide: "Get the next train and get home when I planned, or enjoy a drink and get home 30 or 40 minutes later." I have options. There will always be another train.

1.2 Team-centric: flow the work to the team

Xanpan is team-centric: the team is the production unit, need goes in, working - even valuable - software comes out. This is the machine, the goose that lays the Golden Egg.

Teams everywhere differ: some are large, some are small, some have testers, some don't, some have requirements people, some don't; some are collocated, some are distributed. And some work on one stream of work - call it a 'project' if you will - and some work on multiple streams. In fact, most teams of my experience - both as a team member and an observer - have to deal with multiple streams of work.

Multiple streams might be two projects at once, project A and project B. Or it might be working on a new product while maintaining an old one. Or it might be the team working on project A but individuals being pulled some days to work on something old. These streams might come from different sources, different business units. Or they might come from the same source.

Consequently some work can be known about and planned in advance, and some work just appears, unplanned. There seems to be some unspoken law which mandates that the later work appears, the more urgent it is.

Xanpan aims for stable teams that accept both planned and unplanned work on multiple streams.

1.3 Work to improve Flow

Hand in hand with team-centricity is *flow*. Work arrives at the team from somewhere, somehow. This is inbound flow. Ideally work is flowing into the developer (see Coplien and Harrison 2004 for the Work Flows Inward pattern). Then it has to flow out - perhaps via testers, operations, deployment, and finally to the customer. The actual time needed to do the work may form a very small part of the end-to-end elapsed time.

As with Kanban, Xanpan aims to reduce the overall end-to-end time by improving the flow, making it smoother, more regular, more predictable. Improving flow can also mean levelling flow - reducing the peaks and troughs in work patterns - and constraining work to deliver an overall improvement.

The key to improving flow in Xanpan is allowing work to span more than one iteration. This is heresy in some circles and some texts.

1.4 Quality is free (provided you invest in it)

Philip Crosby wasn't writing about the software industry, but he could have been (Crosby 1980).

There are those in the software industry who believe there is a dial on the wall marked 'Quality'. If you turn the dial down, quality falls and work happens faster. Turn it the other way, dial up quality, and work slows down. They are wrong. This might be true in some industries, but not software.

In software development the dial is wired in reverse: if you want to go fast you dial quality up; when you dial it down, you go slow. Capers Jones has devoted most of his career to studying software development quality and metrics, and he is unambiguous:

> 'Projects with low defect potentials and high defect remove efficiency also have the shortest schedules, lowest costs, and best customer satisfaction levels.' (Jones 2008)

To be clear, when I use the word 'quality' here I am not talking about features, polish, leather upholstery or just about any other external attribute. Indeed I'm not specifically talking about software design or architecture characteristics - although they are implied.

When I say 'quality' I am specifically referring to defects, bugs - or to put it another way: *low quality implies rework* fixes. High quality work does not need rework.

This is not an excuse to gold-plate and over-engineer systems; work may well need to change as we learn things, but we should not be delivering work which quickly requires fixing. All software needs rework. That is the nature of successful software. The question is, how easy is the rework? Low quality makes rework harder, and therefore slower. High quality makes rework easier, and therefore faster.

In the same book Jones says:

'IBM was also the first company to discover that software quality and software productivity were directly coupled and that the project with the lowest defect counts by customers were those with the shortest schedules and the highest development productivity rates. This phenomenon, discovered by IBM in the early 1970s and put in the public domain in May 1975, is still not understood by many other software-producing enterprises that tend to think that quality and productivity are separate issues.' (Jones 2008)

Of course rework occurs not just for defects: requirements changes and unforeseen changes can result in reworking existing code. And ones man's bug is often another's change request. I am perfectly happy to have these debates, but only when a team is approaching zero defects. Until then the team needs to work to improve quality and reduce rework.

Quality is important, because when quality is low there needs to be rework, and when there is significant rework other parts of the Agile jigsaw just don't fit together. High quality is essential to Agile working:

- Rework destroys flow: work must move backwards, work creates work because work creates rework.
- The need for rework means stories and tasks can't truly be considered 'done'.
- When stories aren't truly 'done' iterations are an illusion, because hidden work is flowing between the iterations.
- Metrics are destroyed because work that looks 'done' isn't.

- Developers, testers, managers and others spend inordinate amounts of time prioritising, reporting, managing and even doing rework rather than delivering value.
- Organisations spend inordinate amounts of money on testing resources and cycles: the need for test demonstrates that quality has been sacrificed.

As far as I am concerned anyone who thinks reducing quality is a good way to speed up software development shouldn't be working in the industry.

The need for high quality is why Xanpan embraces all the XP technical practices explicitly. These practices, specifically test-driven development, raise quality, thereby reducing defects and rework. (The software craftsmanship movement continues to advance this cause of quality, and I encourage all to follow the latest thinking here.)

Quality

Any mention of quality, especially high quality, demands a proper discussion of what is quality. Quality will be discussed in more depth in an appendix.

For now when I speak of quality I am essentially speaking of two attributes - *qualities* if you prefer - of a software product:

- Defects: quality is inversely proportional to the number of defects seen in a system, i.e.

lots of defects imply low quality; few (or no)
observed defects do not by themselves imply
high quality, but such a status is a precondition
for high quality.

- Maintainability - changeability and extendibil-
  ity: successful software lives and needs to change
  over time. If software is not changeable, then it
  cannot change as it needs to during its lifetime,
  and it will be hard to remove any defects that
  are found.

There are other attributes that customers, users and
the development team might like to include when
talking about quality for a given product. Indeed
I would encourage all teams to think about what
constitutes quality for their product. However I
believe that these two attributes of quality apply
universally for any software product.

That said, this definition of quality is not a reason to
over-engineer, over-design and gold-plate software.
The Xanpan approach is to achieve these attributes,
not through 'big up-front design', but through repeated design sessions, 'little and often', constant
attention to technical excellence and delivery of
working products in the short term.

Such an approach leads to a form of rework, but this
is rework because things have changed, knowledge

has improved, requirements have changed, new demands have emerged. This is not rework because fault has been found with existing work.

1.5 Visualise

There is surely no team sport in which every player on the field is not accurately aware of the score at any and every moment of play. Yet in software development it is not uncommon to find team members who do not know the next deadline, or what their colleagues are doing. Nor is it uncommon to find managers who have no insight into the work coming their way, or indeed what happens to work when it leaves them.

There are multiple ways in which teams can visualise their work: whiteboards, flip-charts, burn-down charts, cumulative flow diagrams, stickies, posters and many many more.

Software development is an extremely abstract activity. We do things that cause sub-atomic particles to move about in a machine. We work in obscure languages that might look mathematical to some, but look decidedly like natural language to pure mathematicians.

Visualising work helps people learn, it helps people improve flow; visualisation makes it difficult for problems to hide; it creates shared understanding and shared learning. If we cannot see, we cannot learn. If we cannot learn, we are doomed to failure.

1.6 References

Coplien, J. O., and N. B. Harrison. 2004. *Organizational Patterns of Agile Software Development.* Upper Saddle River, NJ: Pearson Prentice Hall.

Crosby, P. B. 1980. *Quality is freeâ€¯: the art of making quality certain.* New American Library.

Jones, C. 2008. *Applied Software Measurement.* McGraw Hill.

2 Board 1

In Xanpan all work is represented on a physical board, usually a magnetic white board, sometimes called a 'Kanban board'. You might decide to use an electronic equivalent, but I always strongly advise teams to start with a physical one until they are familiar working in this way. Working physically is magical - the learning experience is so much stronger and faster. Even if an electronic system is adopted, the team should keep the electronic board publicly visible at all times.

There are many different board designs. Indeed, each team is encouraged to design their own board. Think of this like the light sabres used by Jedi Knights in the 'Star Wars' films: every Jedi must build their own light sabre, and every Xanpan team must design their own board.

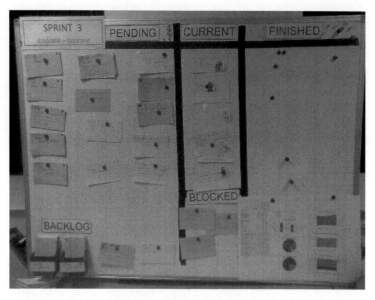

Figure 1 - Basic board design

Figure 1 shows perhaps the most basic board design, and will probably look familiar to many readers. This board is at a laboratory equipment maker in Falmouth (UK). The small - five person - development team creates desktop and embedded software used in products for IVF treatment. In addition they create some embedded software used in the company's own product line facilities.

On the left of the board is the work to be done (the pending column), in the centre is the work in progress (current on this board, commonly known as 'work in progress' or WIP in Kanban), while on the right is the work completed. This photo was taken the day after the team reset the board in the planning meeting, so it is quite clear. Over the course of a sprint, cards move from left to right. The objective is to get as many cards as possible from the left-hand side to the right.

At the bottom left is the 'product backlog'. As with Scrum, the product backlog contains all the work that might be done. In this case the product backlog is physical, and is attached to the board. Personally I like working with a physical backlog, but even I accept it has its limitations. Rows in an Excel spreadsheet can be used, while a GoogleDocs spreadsheet is even better for sharing. Plenty of electronic Agile and 'requirements management' tools are available, but there is value in simplicity.

From the product backlog a subset is selected to do in each sprint. In keeping with Scrum terminology, this is the 'sprint backlog', but may equally be called the 'iteration backlog'. This team has two product backlogs for two 'projects': one embedded, one desktop. In the right-hand corner are graphs showing status. There are actually three burn-down charts here, so the team has three projects in flight. (The third backlog is not visible here for other reasons.)

Each sprint/iteration is two weeks long. They run back-to-back: the end of one sprint is the start of the next. Each sprint begins with an iteration planning meeting and ends with the next such meeting.

In each planning meeting the board is cleared of work done: cards counted, graphs updated, remaining work reviewed and removed if no longer needed, or left if still important. Then the team refill the left-hand side of the board to slightly more than its expected capacity.

This board also shows a blocked column. Whenever the team want to work on a card but cannot - they are blocked - the card is put in the blocked column. This is a signal that escalation may be needed. Or, as in this case, the team is waiting on the customer for additional information before work can continue.

The colour coding of cards is significant. While teams are free to follow their own colour convention, most follow the one laid out in 'blue-white-red':

- Blue cards are development stories - often in user story format, but not always. Blue cards mean something to the business; each card should represent some item of functionality that is valuable to the business/customers.
- White cards are tasks - developer tasks are the most common, but there may be test tasks, analysis tasks or any other type.
- Red cards are bugs - if a problem is found in work done on a white or blue card before the end of the sprint, the card simply moves back to pending or current. If a bug escapes the sprint and a formal bug report is raised, it re-enters the board as a red card.
- Yellow cards are unplanned work. Xanpan allows for both planned and unplanned work. More about these cards in a moment. Bugs requiring an urgent fix may well be unplanned work and should be on the board. Arguably they could be yellow, but red is more commonly used.

Xanpan teams generally follow the Scrum/XP iteration cycle: work is planned in a 'planning meeting' and the team accepts a reasonable amount of work. Unlike Scrum, the team is not asked to commit to performing all the work, neither is the cycle locked; work may continue to enter the sprint.

(The words 'sprint' and 'iteration' are taken to mean exactly the same thing, namely a fixed period of development activity. Scrum introduced the word 'sprint' for this, and Extreme Programming, 'iteration'. In the Xanpan context there is no difference.)

Ideally the team would be able to plan all work up front: no work would be added or removed. However in many environments this is not possible. Bug reports - reds - are one way work may enter. In the case of this team yellows are largely IT support tasks the group needs to look at.

In this picture three IT support yellows are in pending. They have occurred since the start of the sprint, or perhaps they occurred in the last sprint and have been carried over into this one. (Also, unlike Scrum, work can be carried from sprint to sprint: more of this later.) One yellow is in the pending column: someone is actively working on this issue.

While every effort is made to limit work in progress - a default of one task per person - such limits are sometimes broken, and team members need to suspend one task to deal with something more urgent.

Close examination of this picture shows that the yellow in the pending column is on top of a white. One of the developers was working on the white, but has suspended work to deal with an urgent yellow. When this is complete the yellow will be moved to the 'finished' column and work will restart on the white.

Unlike whites, the yellows have no effort estimates. Unlike Kanban, tasks - and perhaps stories - are estimated, most probably using the standard planning poker technique. Yellows are retrospectively estimated by the person who completes the tasks when they move to the finished column.

Red, bugs, may or may not be estimated. They may be estimated in advance - as part of the planning meeting - or retrospectively by the person who undertakes the work. Whether and how they are estimated depends on the team's approach to bugs. The aim is to have no reds - no bugs.

On this board the team has chosen to use Avatars to indicate who is working on which card. Many teams don't bother indicating who is working on what - they remember or don't need to know. Other teams use colour-coded magnets (usually the colour of the magnet is meaningless); one team used coloured star stickers, and another coloured shapes.

Regardless of how or whether the team indicates who is working on what, it is best to avoid allocating work until the last possible moment. This moment is when someone becomes available to work on a task. Ideally the tasks to be done are prioritised. The next time someone finishes a task and becomes available, they simply take the highest-priority task and work on it.

This is the ideal, and it is easy to imagine why this doesn't always happen: someone may lack the skills to work on the next highest task, someone may be working on a related task and it would conflict for two to work on the same thing, and many more reasons.

Allocating tasks as late as possible ensures that priorities are worked on, and reduces bottlenecks around individuals. For this to work, team members need to have similar skill sets.

Most teams - and certainly the team illustrated here - frequently fail to work in strict priority order: however, it should be an aspiration for every team. The first step in this aspiration is to avoid deciding in the planning meeting who will work on each story or task. Instead, wait until at least the daily stand-up meeting, when it becomes clear which stories and tasks will be worked on during the day.

Finally, on this board no attempt is made to indicate how much effort is remaining on a card. The cards have their initial estimates, which are not reduced. It is possible to get an idea of how done a blue is by looking at how many of the associated whites are done, but even this is not very useful. Cards are either done or not done: in programming it is usually impossible to accurately tell how much work is remaining, you don't know when you are about to hit a problem. Therefore we only consider 'done' and 'not-done'.

Similarly there is no attempt to capture 'actual effort' or measure the difference between 'actuals' and estimates. For reasons discussed elsewhere, actuals are only retrospective estimates. When a yellow or red is undertaken without an initial estimate, then a retrospective estimate is put on the card; this is not perfect, but is good enough.

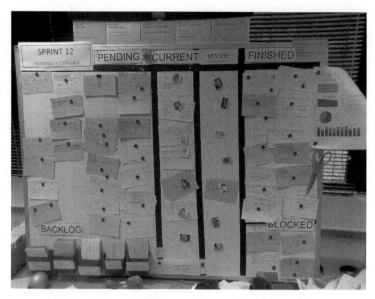

Figure 2 - Basic board five months later

Figure 2 shows the same board five months later. There are fewer yellows in play because the team has hired an IT support engineer to handle most of these tasks. A few support issues or other unplanned work still persist. On the whole support tasks are managed on another board dedicated to the work of the support engineer.

The team has expanded in this picture by joining with a related team that has more engineers and projects (five backlogs now). The merging of the two teams was not entirely successful and was later reversed. The team has added another colour card to the convention: green cards represent process-improvement tasks, perhaps originating in a retrospective, or perhaps from general conversations.

The board has also acquired a new 'review' column. When a card is complete it is first moved here before progressing to the finished column. This serves two purposes: first, to demonstrate what items were completed yesterday when the stand-up meeting is held. Second, it allows the developer to ask for someone else to review the work before it is moved to the finished column, although this is not always necessary.

Key points:

- Cards are colour coded: blue, white, red, yellow and green.
- Iterations/sprints are two weeks in length, and start and end with a planning meeting.
- Xanpan iterations contain both planned and unplanned work.
- The board represent the state of the team and their work, not the state of a particular project.
- The product backlog contains all the work that has been requested for a particular product.
- The sprint backlog contains a subset of the product backlog that is currently in play.
- Xanpan is team-centric, so the team may be working on more than one product or project at a time.
- Estimates are made for work planned in the planning meeting; unplanned work is estimated in retrospect.

3 Iterations

As in XP and Scrum, work is conducted within the framework of time-boxed iterations - also called 'sprints'. These are normally two weeks in length, sometimes one week, sometimes longer, although iterations of three weeks should be avoided. Iterations of four weeks or more, while once common, are often seen as as too long now.

Changes to iteration length should be rare. Teams may occasionally decide to move, say, from two-week iterations to one-week iterations, or to four-week iterations. Once changed, the team will stay in this mode for several iterations before considering another change.

Ad hoc changes to iteration length should be avoided, although at times such as Christmas it might make sense to suspend iterations, or have just one iteration of a longer length then usual.

What is not allowed is extending an iteration by a few days because the work planned for the iteration has not been finished. Not only does this disrupt the following iteration, it also destroys the value of doing work in iterations in the first place. It destroys the deadline effect, it destroys benchmarking, and it negates the 'get good at doing things in short bursts' ethos.

Having to work to a deadline not only focuses individuals' attention, it also limits the work in progress, forces teams to address problems that might otherwise be hidden, and stops procrastination. People are actually quite good at working to deadlines.

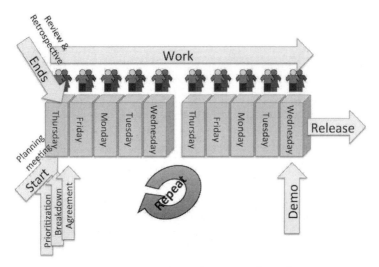

Figure 3 - Typical 2 week iteration (sprint)

The next iteration starts immediately after the previous one ends. Often the end of iteration meeting for one iteration simply flows into the planning meeting for the next iteration. The planning meeting (described below) marks the start of the next iteration. During the meeting the board is reset for the next iteration of work. Once the planning meeting is complete, work begins.

The first big difference with Xanpan iterations compared with Scrum or some other methods is that work can, and does, flow between iterations. Taking work into an iteration does not mean that the team is in any way committed to doing the work.

During the end of iteration review, work still in the 'to do' section of the board is examined and may be returned to the backlog, or removed (de-scoped) completely if the team and Product Owner agree. In most cases though work remains in 'to do' and is simply left in play and carried to the next iteration, forming the starting point of planning.

The second major difference from Scrum is that Xanpan allows both planned and unplanned work. If teams can plan all the work for the next two weeks and stick to the planned work, great; if not, then the team accepts the work and does it. By tracking the planned versus unplanned work, this can be factored into forecasts.

Xanpan differs from Scrum on this point for several reasons:

- Allowing work to flow from iteration to iteration creates Kanban-style flow mechanics.
- Forcing stories to be small enough to fit within an iteration regularly results in stories that are too small to have any business value - especially for teams new to iterations. It is more important that a story delivers business value than that it fits in an iteration.
- Over time teams will get better at slicing stories small enough to fit into an iteration and big enough to have value. Over time the team will get better at delivering stories in one iteration. However, this is hard when a team is moving to iterative working.
- Teams in some domains, such as embedded and telecoms, or using some technologies, such as C++, and those working with unfamiliar, often legacy systems, find it harder to reconcile small stories with business value.

- Rather than use Scrum style commitment, teams are encouraged to try and do more work than they expect to do, and it is accepted that not all work taken into the iteration will get done. There is little to lose by trying for more. Statements about what will be delivered at the end of the iteration are statements of probability, e.g. "The highest priority story is almost certain to be delivered, the next is probable, the next maybe and the last unlikely."

In an ideal world a team would size every story to fit within an iteration and deliver value. Teams are encouraged to aim for this. But even here there is a problem:

> Assume there are two stories: A and B; each will take 7 of the 10 working days in the sprint. Both are acceptable: the team starts on A and completes it as expected. On day 8 the team is ready for a new story. Do they pick up B? Some Scrum teams would not, as they may never have scheduled the work in the first place. At some point, in planning or when A is done, they will look for a piece of work that is 2 days long.

This is the Scrum equivalent of dry-stone walling. A suitable story may not exist: even if it does, who is to say it is a priority? Why wouldn't the team start on the next highest priority story rather than go hunting through the low priorities for one that happens to be the right size?

3.1 Releasable

The key point about the end of the iteration is that the team should have a releasable product. This does not mean that the product is released: hopefully it is, or it moves straight to release after the end of the iteration. Essentially whether a product is released at the end of an iteration or not is a business - most likely a marketing - decision. At the end of every iteration the team gives the business an opportunity to release the product as is.

When work flows from iteration to iteration regularly there should always be some stories that are completed in an iteration even if some are carried over. Occasionally there may be an iteration where nothing is complete; this isn't good, but it might happen. If it happens regularly then there is probably a problem that needs to be addressed.

Increasingly teams are not only practising continuous integration, but continuous deployment. As work is ready it is pushed to release. When teams get good at doing two-week releases, this is a logical next step. This mandates that each story - each blue - is in its own right releasable.

3.2 Iteration sequence

Although an iteration follows the same basic sequence as a Scrum or Extreme Programming iteration for completeness, it is best to talk through the iteration.

An iteration starts with a planning meeting; these are described in detail in the next chapter. During this meeting the Product

Owner will present the work they would like done in the next iteration. This work should be presented in absolute priority order - 1, 2, 3, ... - no Moscow rules, no equal priority.

The development team will break this work down into tasks. The team and Product Owner then need to reach agreement on what will be done. Xanpan uses a variation of the XP velocity system to gauge how much work the team should achieve. Teams are advised to accept slightly more work than they expect to do, but to expectation-manage the message. Nothing is guaranteed, so it is important that those who want to know what the iteration will produce understand that some things are more likely than others, and some things won't be delivered.

Once the iteration planning meeting is complete, work begins. Each day - preferably first thing in the morning - the team hold a stand-up meeting of no more than 15 minutes to synchronise and share their progress and issues. Ideally no other meetings are needed.

At the end of the iteration the team should at the very least undertake a demonstration to stakeholders. It might well be that the Product Owner has seen the work, as it is completed and has no need for a demonstration: they may even be the one running the demonstration.

The best teams will go straight to release - after the demo or perhaps skipping the demo altogether - as the iteration closes. It is then time for the review and retrospective.

The review is purely a bookkeeping exercise: count the cards and points, update any tracking systems, file any reports and so on. Retrospectives are intended to help the team improve their working in the next and subsequent iterations.

Retrospectives may be as informal as a once-around-the-table opportunity for everyone to say how they thought the last iteration went and what they suggest for the next one. Alternatively, they may be formal, with set exercises such as dialogue sheets (http://www.dialoguesheets.com) or from a book (e.g. Derby and Larsen 2006; Kerth 2001).

With the retrospective complete, it is time for the next iteration planning meeting. There might be a lunch or coffee break between the two meetings, but there is no need for a lot more.

3.3 Mid-week to mid-week

Figure 3 deliberately shows an iteration running mid-week to mid-week. My experience, and the experience of others assisting teams, is that running iterations mid-week to mid-week is more effective than running them Monday to Friday. Why this should be so is difficult to pin down, but there are several reasons that I believe contribute:

- The 'Friday afternoon effect'. If an iteration resets on a Monday, then anyone completing a piece of work on Friday will not be particularly motivated to start another piece of work. In many environments it is common to finish early on Friday, or take a long lunch. If the iteration has several more days to run, there is less incentive to 'slack off' on a Friday afternoon.
- Monday refresh. I believe there is research showing that people are more effective at the start of a new week. I hasten to add I have not read this research myself, which

is a little lax of me. Anecdotally many people, if asked, say their most productive day is Tuesday. Assuming there is truth in these tales, it is a good reason to avoid meetings on Monday and Tuesday.

- Public holidays. In the UK and many other countries many public holidays occur on Mondays. This means that there is more chance of an iteration meeting being disrupted if it is scheduled on a Monday.
- Personal holidays. Again in the UK and many other countries individuals are more likely to take a Friday or Monday off as a long weekend. Consequently planning meetings on these days are more likely to be missing a team member.
- Meeting rooms. In a surprising number of organisations booking a meeting room can be difficult, either because there is a shortage of rooms or the booking process is complex. Therefore it is worth striving to book rooms further in advance on a regular basis, and minimise changes. Indeed, it can be impossible to book a meeting room in some companies for the day after a public holiday, because all the meeting conveners are trying to move their meetings back one day.
- Regular schedule. Keeping to a very regular schedule has many benefits, one of which is that meeting rooms can be booked weeks, months, even years in advance. If you have an electronic booking system, set the meeting to repeat with no end date.
- Time zones. Although it is best to collocate teams, many find this is not an option. A team in Holland has programmers in Houston; a team in London has analysts in New York, a team in Pennsylvania has members in Bangalore

and so on. Thus holding any whole team meeting means someone may need to work late or arrive early. Asking team members to work late on a Friday, or arrive early on a Monday, encroaches on family time and space.

There are probably more reasons that could be added to this list. None is in itself conclusive, and you might choose to argue with some of the points. As I said, experience - not theory - shows mid-week to mid-week is best. Perhaps the best advice is to experiment for yourself.

3.4 Iteration length

The default length of an iteration is two weeks. You need a pretty good reason to do anything different. If in doubt, do one-week iterations at first. You may later extend them to two weeks or four weeks.

I find monthly iterations to be too long. Remember that software has diseconomies of scale: pushing up to a month allows too much to change, and means that too much needs to be planned and scheduled in a planning meeting.

There are natural human rhythms and rituals based on weekly, fortnightly and monthly iterations. The working week is a week long, many people take two weeks for their summer holidays, the lunar month is almost 28 days. I have never heard of a natural cycle that takes 21 days. In English and many other languages there are words for these time-frames: week, fortnight and month. What we do not have is a word for a three-week period - and I have yet to find a language that does! It is hard to think of any human or natural cycle that takes 21 days to complete. Yet it is not uncommon to come across teams that run three-week iterations. Usually these teams exist within a corporate IT environment, and it is not uncommon to find mini-waterfall processes within the three-week iteration.

Typically when asked "Why did you choose three weeks?", they reply "Because we don't think we could do anything useful in two weeks". This misses an important point of short iterations: they exist to make you better.

Working in short iterations has many benefits: predictability and routine, reference benchmarking and more. However the iterations themselves are not the biggest benefit. The biggest benefit comes from the changes that need to be made, the problems that need to be resolved, the processes that need to be changed, and so on, in order to work effectively in short iterations.

Iterations are not an end in their own right - rather they are a tool for making you better. Forcing yourself - and others, processes, tools and so on - to produce something useful, valuable, in two weeks, forces change for the better.

A team that is just starting with Agile is well advised to start with one-week iterations in order to practise the starting and stopping activities, see problems and resolve them.

3.5 Release schedules

Many teams will synchronise software releases with the iteration, so a new version of the software appears every two weeks. Better still, individual blue cards would be releasable, so the team could release multiple times during an iteration. Stories of Kanban, XP or Scrum teams releasing many times during a week are increasingly common: this is the start of 'continuous deployment'.

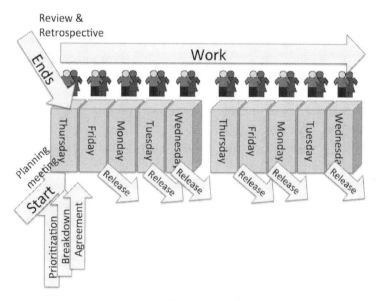

Iteration with multiple releases

Before trying for releases during the iteration, a team need to be capable of releasing at the end of the iteration (or even releasing at all). For a team which currently finds it difficult to release the first objective is to be able to release every two weeks. Once this can be done fairly painlessly they can then consider more frequent, even smaller, releases.

For every team releasing during an iteration there are probably more teams releasing at the end. And, as far as I can see, there are more still who release after several iterations. For example, six two-week iterations followed by a quarterly release used to be fairly common. Releasing every second iteration, so once a month, is also common.

I myself ran a team that made one monthly release after four one-week iterations. Occasionally there was a fifth iteration to stay with the publicised release schedule of 'first Tuesday of the month'. The first planning meeting of the new cycle was longer than the subsequent ones. While features did change, it was broadly possible to see what was coming for the next month and work on the details iteration by iteration.

3.6 The CEO test

Imagine you have just finished an iteration, perhaps yesterday or the day before yesterday. The CEO walks in and says "Bad news, we are out of money, we can't make payroll". While you are taking in this shocking statement he adds "Of course, if you have something I can release today, we can get some revenue and we have another month".

If your answer is "Sure, here's one we just finished", then everything is OK.

If on the other hand your answer is "Well we just finished something, we are code complete on some stories, but we need another month or two of test-fix-test-fix", then you are out of work and out of pocket.

Never be tempted to do more work which looks done but isn't. Get good at finishing things completely, to release standard. Do fewer features and more quality.

Do this and you not only give your CEO options - you change the game.

3.7 References

Derby, E., and D. Larsen. 2006. *Agile Retrospectives*. Pragmatic Programmers.

Kerth, N. L. 2001. *Project Retrospectives*. New York: Dorset House.

4 Planning Meetings

One of the things I enjoy about my work as a consultant on Agile is visiting teams and observing iteration planning meetings. If you've never observed another team's planning meeting, or if you've never seen one, you might expect them to be fairly similar. Indeed they are but, as is so often the case, the devil is in the detail. I am routinely surprised by the ability of teams to interpret, find and invent different ways to doing things in the meeting.

Take for example deciding how much work a team can undertake. Some teams just have the product owner propose stories and accept stories until they feel they have 'enough'. Some teams are strict in only accepting stories they are sure they can get done - the Scrum idea of 'commitment'; other teams will take on more work than they expect to do.

Some teams will use velocity to judge how much they can do. They determine how many points they can do at the start of the planning meeting and then accept stories up to that limit, give or take a bit. Some teams set the upper limit by simply looking at how many points they did last time and rolling that forward, called 'yesterday's weather' in XP. Some teams play planning poker to decide how many points they can do. Some teams think about who's on holiday, who's not, who was ill, what got in the way and a million other things.

Seeing these variations is often educational for me, and vice versa, I sometimes suggest changes to a team's current practice.

However it does mean that when describing a planning meeting to someone, there are a lot of details that could be different without necessarily being wrong.

Personally I advise teams not to spend a lot of time deciding how many points they can do. I don't see much point in asking "Who's in this week" or "Who is out?". You could add more and more detail without adding any more accuracy. All the team needs is a rough guide to judge how much work it is worth planning in detail.

To keep it simple, I would say just take the average velocity from the last four or five sprints, and ignore holidays, illness and other factors that might have, or will, disrupt work. Recalculate this average at the start of each iteration, i.e. use a rolling average.

Then - and this is both important and slightly controversial - schedule slightly more work than the team expects to do. That is, if the team expects to do 10 points, then schedule 12 or 13. If they expect to do 20, schedule 24 or 25.

The team needs to accept enough work that it doesn't run out of things to do, but should not accept more than is reasonable to expect. Preparing work that will not get done is wasteful.

What follows is my take on a planning meeting and how it runs. This description matches the A1 Planning Sheet

After this description I detail some of the activities which might occur outside the planning meeting but which contribute to a smooth running planning meeting.

I will also detail some variations I've seen.

4.1 The Players

- The *Product Owner*: this role is usually played by a product manager, or a business analyst acting as a proxy for the real customer. On occasions the real customer might play the role. Some companies employ subject matter experts who can play the role of Product Owner at times. Sometimes someone else needs to play the role. Whoever plays Product Owner needs to do their homework (see below) and be ready to propose stories, answer questions, prioritise and make decisions as the meeting progresses.

  While it is common practice for there to be only one Product Owner, there may be more than one. If more than one Product Owner (for the same product) attends the planning meeting, they should agree priorities and approaches beforehand .

- The *Creators*: software engineers and testers mainly, although sometimes others, such as user interface designers, are involved. These are the people who will build the things the Product Owner asks for.
- The *Facilitator*: sometimes there is a dedicated facilitator who is not the Product Owner or a member of the building team. They may be, for example, a project manager, Scrum master or Agile coach.

  Some teams are too small to have a dedicated facilitator, so a developer steps into the role - in which case they wear two hats during the meeting.

Experienced teams may not need a facilitator, but inexperienced teams who lack a facilitator may find the meetings long and difficult. Whoever plays facilitator should have some experience of planning meetings and facilitation. They should also have respect and authority from the team to play the role.

Usually it is not a good idea for the Product Owner to double up as facilitator, because someone needs to watch for and resolve disputes between the Product Owner and developers. The Product Owner usually has more than enough to do during the planning meeting in any case.

I consider the total of all the people in these roles, and possibly some more as well, to be: the development team. The Product Owner and facilitator are, in my book, as much part of the team as the coders and testers.

4.2 The Artefacts

There are several artefacts, or props, which are normally used in a planning meeting. When teams rehearse planning meetings in training courses, I use dice to simulate the work in an iteration. While dice are not used in real-life planning meetings, they do simulate the nature variability that occurs in reality.

- *Blue cards*: describe bits of functionality that are useful to the business in a language the business representatives

understand. These are vertical slices of business functionality that are conceivably deliverable on their own. Often
a 'user story' format (Cohn 2004) is used and the cards are
usually created before the planning meeting.

- *White cards*: each card describes one task needed in building the thing described on the blue card. White cards are
normally written during the planning meeting, and there
are usually multiple white task cards for each blue card.
- *Red Cards*: these are bugs and other expedited items.
Normally reds are not broken down into tasks, but they are
occasionally. What colour you use for tasks related to a red
card is up to you: white or red would both be appropriate.
- *Planning board*: usually a magnetic white board divided
into columns. Often these boards are 1.2m by 90cm but the
size is part particularly important, other sizes and types
of boards may be used. While many teams use electronic
tracking systems, I strongly advise teams initially to adopt
physical boards and cards, and only progress to electronic
systems when they have some physical experience. Even
then both systems may be run in parallel.
- *Planning poker cards*: the description that follows assumes
the team is playing planning poker. Not all teams play
planning poker; it isn't compulsory, so feel free to use
whatever method works for you. That said, whatever
method you use should address some of the point discussed below.

Special sets of planning poker cards are available - these can be
surprising difficult to buy, but are often freely available from
Agile training and consulting companies - just ask! Different
planning poker sets have slightly different sequences.

The exact colour of the story and task cards can vary from team to team. Keeping to the colours outlined here does keep things consistent.

Some teams use additional colours to signal other types of work. One team started using yellow cards to signal unplanned work; this Xanpan convention has been described elsewhere. By their nature yellow cards will only appear at a planning meeting when they represent carry-over work.

4.3 The Meeting Sequence

The basic format of the meeting is shown in the diagram below. The team agree how much work they will attempt, the Product Owner presents the work they would like done and the team works through each item in priority order. They discuss each item, break it down to tasks and estimate the tasks.

After each item is done (i.e. discussion and breakdown has ended) team members count up how much work they have accepted and compare this with what they expect to do. If they have spare capacity, the next highest priority item is pulled from the Product Owner and the discussion, breakdown and estimation process repeats.

When the team has accepted work to its capacity, its members review what they have with the Product Owner and agree any changes.

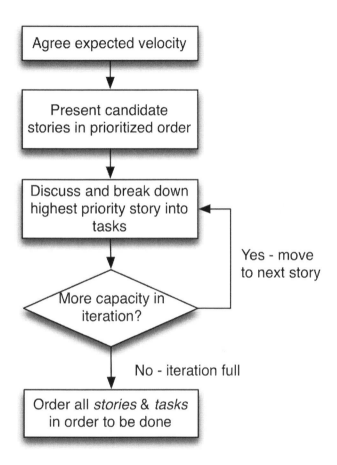

Figure 4 - Basic meeting sequence

First meeting

The first planning meeting a team holds is always the hardest. This is when their experience is least and the unknowns greatest;

naturally it will take longer to navigate the meeting. In the worst cases the team's lack of experience can derail the meeting altogether should it encounter difficulties.

The first meeting is also the most difficult for another reason: the team has no reference points. They have little idea of what they need from a story, how long it will take to do a story, or quite what acceptance criteria should look like. Even if they have practised for these questions during training, doing it in real life will be harder.

Significantly the team will also have no data on how fast it can go - it will only have a vague idea of how big 'one point' is or how many points it should accept into an iteration. In my experience teams tend to accept far more work into the first sprint than they will ever get done: they are inherently optimistic.

Second and subsequent

Because the first meeting takes so long and over-plans, the second meeting, two weeks later, tends to be one of the shortest. So much work is carried over in one form or another that the second meeting finds little to plan. After that the meetings start to settle down. The team has two meetings under its belt and two data points.

The meeting format also changes after the first meeting. At first the meeting is entirely forward-looking, but subsequent meetings have a backward-looking element. Prior to the start of the meeting, or right at the start, the team will demonstrate the work done in the previous iteration. It will then review the work done, usually by counting the points and updating any charts.

Formally the demonstration, review and retrospective might be separate meetings. But they are likely to be arranged back-to-back, perhaps with a short break between each. So whether one regards them as one long meeting or several shorter meetings is debatable.

When teams only delivered at the end of iteration - or less regularly - the demonstration of developed functionality used to be an essential part of the end-of-iteration and start of the next iteration. As more teams move to continuous delivery, it is worth questioning whether the demo adds anything if people can already use the actual software.

Teams may also hold a retrospective as part of the iteration end routine, although not all teams hold retrospectives, and even those who do may not hold them at every iteration.

The schedule of the second and subsequent meetings is something like the diagram below.

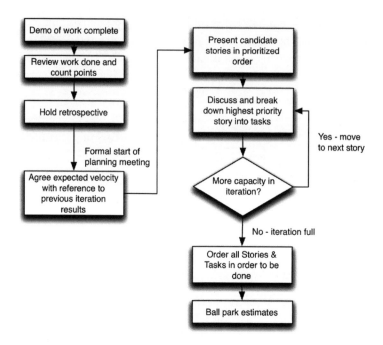

Figure 5 - Subsequent meeting sequence

In the second meeting the team has a rough idea of how many points of work it can accept, because members can sum up the points completed in the previous iteration. In the third meeting it has a better idea because it can average points from two iterations. By the fourth meeting the average is fairly accurate, plus reasonable high water (best case) and low water (worse case) marks can guide capacity thinking.

These meetings should happen regularly at the end/start of every iteration - typically every two weeks. They can be scheduled in everyone's calendar and room bookings made months in advance. If you are using an electronic scheduling system (such as Microsoft Outlook) you can set up a recurring meeting with no end date.

4.4 The Planning Game

The game opens with the Product Owner(s) presenting to the team the blue (business facing) stories they wish to have developed. These are presented in absolute priority order - 1, 2, 3, 4 etc. No duplicate priorities are allowed, i.e. there can be only one priority one, one priority two and so on.

If two items are deemed to be of equal priority by the Product Owner (e.g. two cards are both assigned priority three), then the development team is allowed to decide the ordering. If the Product Owner disagrees with the ordering then they have, by their disagreement, determined the ordering. In general it is considered an abdication of responsibility if a Product Owner does not guide the team in prioritisation.

Each blue card is broken down by the development team to a set of white technical tasks. The white cards describe the things that need to be done in order to build the blue. One might think of the whites as the building blocks for the blues, or of the whites as *verbs* and blues as *nouns*.

Blues are the domain of the Product Owner, whites of the technical team. The breakdown is partly an act of design, partly an act of requirements elaboration, and partly an act designed to produce the smallest practical work items. (I will discuss the breakdown in more detail later.)

Of course sometimes only one white is needed to create one blue. In these cases the white is omitted and the team can work directly at the blue level. In some ways this represents the idea scenario; however, for this to work, the blue must be no bigger than one white, i.e. if the blue can be broken down to multiple whites, it should be. (Of course there comes a point where further breakdown is excessive, but to start with teams find breakdown difficult. Once they have mastered it, they might consider whether some tasks are too small.)

The breakdown is a cooperative process between the development team and Product Owner - both should be present. There should be conversation between both sides: developers should ask about the requirements in detail, Product Owners may promote white cards to blue cards if they think the task itself has business value, and remove technical tasks if they want - even against the advice of developers - although in general the two sides should strive for consensus.

Giving Product Owners the ability to promote whites to blues can be a useful tool in extracting business value. It also gives the Product Owner the power to override much of the technical team's advice. On occasion this may be useful, but it may also indicate problems. For example, a Product Owner who frequently finds whites to promote may not be devoting the time and attention to preparing small blues in advance. Or it may be a sign that they do not trust the technical team and are attempting to micro-manage the work.

When white task cards have been broken out, those who will be responsible for undertaking the work - i.e. development team, all developers and testers, but not the Product Owner - estimate the work in terms of abstract points using Planning Poker. (See discussion below).

Teams track velocity from iteration to iteration. Unlike in financial services, past performance is considered a good indicator of future performance, or at least of the next iteration. I normally recommend using a rolling average across the last four or five iterations to judge upcoming capacity.

Once breakdown of a blue has started, it makes sense to see it through to the end. Even if part way through the team realise they cannot fit the tasks into this iteration, it probably doesn't make sense to stop mid-breakdown. This might result in the team accepting more work than it planned to, but this isn't a problem, as there is no commitment.

Of course once it becomes clear that a blue will not be completed in the iteration, the Product Owner could drop the blue and suggest a substitute. There is no hard and fast rule here. It makes little sense to plan the first tasks for a blue, but the order in which tasks are done does not necessarily correspond to the order in which they were identified and written on whites.

The team may or may not achieve all the scheduled work; they may perform below or above expected velocity in any given iteration. If the team do more then expected than the work is available, and over time the rolling average used to calculate the expected velocity will rise. Conversely, if the team find the iteration harder than expected, then less will be achieved and, after a couple of iteration, the rolling average will fall.

If a particular task or feature must be achieved within the iteration, it should be scheduled first and within the minimum recent velocity, low-water mark. This does not guarantee that the work will be done, but provides a very high probability. Teams are advised to track the time it takes for cards to traverse the tracking board and develop statistically reliable averages and deviations to replace the Planning Poker estimation process.

Testing

Different teams handle testing in different ways. Some teams have professional testers and formal test processes, while some teams have neither. The level of automated testing is also widely different between teams.

White cards are generally not testable by professional testers. They should be tested by developers using automated unit tests and other tools to ensure they are acceptable. If there is something a tester could test, they may well be involved.

Generally professional testers work at the blue card level. In work breakdown a team might write a white task card to test a blue. This card would only be done once all the other whites were done and the whole blue was ready to test.

However, testers may prefer to write two task cards: one to write the test script and one to execute the test. If the former is fully automated, the latter need not exist, or will happen automatically.

Other teams forego tasks associated with testing and instead model tests via their task board. As cards move across the board they will need to pass through test columns where the testing will happen. Thus completion of all the white cards associated with a blue would trigger the move of the blue into a testing column and for testing to commence.

Trivia and Spikes

Truly trivial tasks, or work to be undertaken by people outside the teams, may be assigned zero points. Such zero-point cards represent work that the team needs to keep track of but which does not represent noticeable work for the team. For example, a 'buy domain name' task would probably merit a zero-point score, as it would take about 10 minutes. But a task of 'Obtain quote for domain name, seek approval to spend money, buy domain name, file expenses claim' may warrant an estimate larger than zero.

Spike cards are written when the development team feel they do not have enough knowledge - usually technical knowledge - to begin a breakdown and estimate. Here a spike card will be written to attempt the work, but once the work is done it will be thrown away, spiked.

The objective of a spike card is to gain an understanding of what needs to be done. Typically the output from a spike will be a set of (white) cards describing the tasks which need to be done. Ideally these cards will be held until the next planning meeting, where they can be discussed, estimated and scheduled, or deferred.

Sometimes when time is pressing the resulting cards might be estimated and scheduled into the iteration immediately. While this is entirely practical, it does mean forecasts for what the iteration will produce are difficult or impossible.

Spikes are not estimated in the same way that other cards are estimated - rather they are hard time-boxed: an amount of time is decided on and written on the card. This time, no more, no less, is the time allowed for this card. When the time is up research work must stop and the task cards must be written using the knowledge gained.

Working in time - as opposed to points - for spikes makes velocity calculations more difficult. Some approximate, rule-of-thumb, back-of-the-envelope calculations need to be done in order to apportion a number of points to a time-boxed spike card.

Counting 'Done'

In the review part of the meeting the work completed in the previous iteration is removed from the board and reviewed. The main part of this review is simply counting the points done and updating any charts or other tracking systems. The review may also take time to examine any cards left on the board and decide whether they should be left as carry-over.

Teams are encouraged to adopt a definition of 'done' to help with defining what is *done* and what is *not done*. The definition of 'done' is a short checklist of things the team agree will be *done* for every card they claim is 'done'. This checklist applies to all cards in addition to any acceptance criteria placed on blues.

I normally recommend a definition of 'done' for whites' tasks, although some teams also apply it to blues. Occasionally teams feel the need for one definition for blues and another for whites.

The estimated points on completed whites are counted as part of the team's iteration velocity. Only 100%-completed whites are counted and the estimate is counted as-is, even if people feel it does not reflect the actual work. For example, if a card is estimated at five points it is counted as five points, regardless of whether people feel it was actually closer to one or 10.

No attempt is made to capture or work with 'actual' time or points. Human perception of 'how long things take' is subjective, and Vierordt's Law suggests we underestimate retrospectively as well as prospectively. The historical velocity data provides the necessary feedback on how long things took. By allowing abstract points to 'float', the system becomes self-adjusting.

Anyone who has worked with software teams for more than a few years will have seen the '80% done' scenario in which a piece of work remains 80% done for 80% of the time allowed. Therefore no matter how much a developer claims that "It is 95% done", incomplete cards are not counted.

In software development we have no way of telling objectively what is 95% done and what is 9% done. We have no way of knowing if an unexpected problem lurks in the final 5%, or if someone will go ill before the day is out.

This rule also sets up a small incentive for people to complete work before the end of iteration review and thus score more points. This adds a little extra motivation.

When an average velocity is used it becomes unimportant - for capacity measurement - exactly for which iteration the points are scored. Suppose a 10-point card is genuinely 90% done in iteration 13, but is not counted. It is then completed early in iteration 14, and thus counted in that iteration. While the variability of velocity will increase iteration-to-iteration, the effect of averaging over several sprints will still allow reasonable planning. The aim of estimation and forecasting is not to be precise about any single item, but to be generally accurate.

I just don't believe that adjusting for 'actuals' on a card-by-card basis, or allowing some points from partially done cards to be counted, is a productive use of time. Both are subjective measures that invite discussion and disagreement - both time-consuming activities.

Some see it as odd that I allow whites to be counted even when blues are not. "But the business functionality is incomplete", they say, "and it's the business need that counts". This is reasonable - and certainly follows the rules of Scrum - but I find it leads to less predictability in the process and evens out flow.

Counting whites as they are completed smoothes the flow. Only counting blues will lead to more variability, higher peaks and deeper troughs. While this complicates planning, it does not undermine it. One team I know of only counted points when blues were done, and they still delivered on time.

As before, the use of averages means that if a team decides to count only points from completed blues rather than whites, the velocity benchmarking system will still work. The drawback is that it might take slightly longer to stabilise and provide a stable capacity benchmark.

4.5 Velocity and currency

Velocity is a measure of how fast a team is working, or rather, how much work it is getting through. It is calculated by counting the points a team scored (i.e. completed) in the previous iteration.

Over a series of several iterations, say four, a team should be able to come up with a rolling average, a high- and a low-water mark which can be used for planning purposes. For example, consider the team shown in this graph:

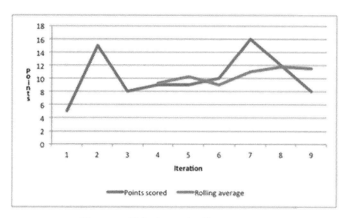

Figure 6 - Velocity and rolling average

This team scored 5, 15, 8, 9, 9, 10, 16, 12 and 8 points in the nine iterations shown here. At the end of iteration four the team could calculate an average of the last four iterations; this could be rolled forward at the end of each iteration, giving rolling averages of 9.25, 10.25, 9, 11, 11.75 and 11.5.

I would advise the team to plan for 12 points of work (because their recent average is 11.5) but accept 16 or 17 points worth - up to their recent high-water mark. Those in the planning meeting will be aware of the possible outcomes, but for those outside the meeting there needs to be some management of expectations.

It is pretty much certain the team will achieve the first 8 points worth of work. The team might get points 9 to 12 done, or they might not. If they are very lucky they will do points 13 to 16.

If someone needs to know how much time the team spent on a particular task, then it is simply a question of maths. Assume there are five developers employed for 40 hours a week in the previous example. That is 200 hours of work, producing on average slightly more than 11 points of work, so each point took on average a little over 18 hours, thus a two-point card took about 36 hours.

I would prefer not to make this calculation too well known, because once it entered general knowledge it will undermine the points system. I would also prefer that this calculation be regularly updated since, as shown in the table, the averaging changes.

It is vital to note that points float. Like the US Dollar, Euro or Pound Sterling, points are a currency and change their value over time. Each team has its own currency that is not directly transferable to another team.

As with currencies and other economic indicators, setting targets for velocity can create problems. Goodhart's Law applies: if a team tries to target a certain number of points, it will meet its goal, but may not do any more work. Such teams exhibit inflation in estimates: exactly as with financial inflation, the numbers are bigger but the value less. (More about Goodhart's Law later, or see http://en.wikipedia.org/wiki/Goodharts_law).

Carry-over work

For a strict Scrum team there is no issue of work carry-over, because teams only commit to work they guarantee will be done, and thus all work committed to is done. While many Scrum teams find carrying work over from sprint-to-sprint an anathema, I advise teams to carry over work. Indeed, carrying over work to improve flow is a central feature of Xanpan.

For Xanpan teams work carry-over is a fact of life. As part of the review process preceding the planning meeting the team should look at the work remaining on the board from the closing iteration and decide which, if any, work will be carried over to the next iteration.

When work has not started on a blue and associated whites, the Product Owner may decide to pull the card completely or roll the whole thing over. Assuming they roll it over, it will need to be prioritised against the new blues being added. That is to say, just because a blue is rolled over does not give it special priority.

When some tasks associated with a blue have been done and some tasks have not the situation is more complicated. While the Product Owner may still pull the blue or assign it a low priority, it probably makes more sense to finish work that has been started, and finish it soon, rather than leaving it in a partially done state.

There may also be engineering reasons why the blue should be taken to completion before anything else. For example, some of the new blues may involve the same areas of code.

In a few cases work is incomplete because more tasks came to light after it began. While I do not allow teams to change estimates on whites once they are accepted into an iteration, the team may write new whites for additional work which emerged. They may even estimate and begin work on these whites during the iteration if need be. However I prefer it if new work can be held until the planning meeting, where it can be discussed, prioritised and scheduled by the team.

Obviously this approach raises the possibility of never-ending work, blues that are never done. Senior team members need to be watchful for this and work to diagnose the underlying issues causing it.

How long is a planning meeting?

I would expect a well-practised team to complete a planning meeting in half a day; my preference is for afternoon meetings. Obviously there is some variability, depending on how big the team is, how much work is being planned and whether the team is carrying over any work, but half a day should be enough.

The exception is the first meeting, which will frequently take much longer, perhaps as much as a day. Meetings can also stretch out when Product Owners are poorly prepared for the meeting or take issue with estimates. Design questions can also derail meetings, but on the whole most design issues can be followed up later.

A team holding a retrospective before the meeting should allow 60 to 90 minutes, depending on the techniques and exercises being used. I find a dialogue sheet retrospective takes 60 minutes for the sheet, plus up to 30 minutes for post-sheet discussion and action items.

4.6 Product Owner Preparations (Homework)

One of the recurring reasons I see for planning meetings not going smoothly is a lack of preparation on the part of the Product Owner. The planning meeting is not the place for the Product Owner to decide what is required. Although they may make trade-offs and substitutions during the meeting, they need to go into the meeting knowing very clearly what they want to ask for. This does not mean everything they want will be accepted and scheduled, but they should be prepared.

The Product Owner needs to be on top of their brief: they need to be able to answer developer questions and clarify what is being asked for. If they cannot, they need to either bring someone who can, or be prepared to make changes to what they want. Thus, if the testers and developers ask questions about issues the Product Owner cannot answer immediately, they might bring another story into play while they find out the answers. This may mean that the first story is postponed until the following iteration - or even later - or it may be possible to schedule the difficult story later in the iteration.

As you might guess from this, it helps if the Product Owner is not only prepared for the iteration they are planning now, but also has a rough idea of what they plan to ask for in future iterations. These plans shouldn't be too detailed - because things change both in priority and detail - but the Product Owner needs to have some ideas.

Medium-term plans, about the next few iterations, were traditionally called *release plans*. I believe the name *quarterly plans* both better describes the plan and moves away from the association with releases. (This is discussed in a later section, *Planning Beyond the Iteration*.)

It is also critical that the Product Owner has authority from the organisation and team to make decisions during the planning meeting: on priorities, on changes to priorities, on details of features and on trade-offs. Nothing is more disruptive - and morale-sapping - than completing a planning meeting one day only to discover a day or two later that somebody else has overruled the Product Owner and has changed what was agreed in the meeting.

There is sometimes a need to have more than one Product Owner in the planning meeting. When this happens all Product Owners concerned need to be in agreement about what is going to be asked for and what the priorities are, and be prepared for problems. The Product Owners may benefit from having their own small meeting prior to the full planning meeting.

> An Iteration Planning Sheet is available to accompany this description. Visit http://www.softwarestrategy.co.uk/dlgsheets/planningsheet.html to download a sheet or to buy a printed sheet.

4.7 References

Cohn, M. 2004. *User Stories Applied.* Addison-Wesley.

5 More Planning and Estimation

The previous chapters have described workflow in general - iterations and planning meetings. In this chapter I'd like to go into some of the issues mentioned in more depth and set out the rationale for running the system in the way I've suggested. As a result this chapter is a little bit of a hotchpotch of ideas, and you may want to skip some sections.

5.1 Ballpark estimates

Point estimation and velocity can result in a reliable, predictable system. However it sometimes helps to have a rough idea of what is coming up, how big items might be, without spending time breaking work down.

It makes sense to delay breakdown - from blue to white - for as long as possible. If breakdown occurs early work might go away or change, rendering the breakdown irrelevant and wasteful. Early breakdown itself delays the doing of the work and of other work.

More importantly, early breakdown means that the team breaks down work when it knows less about the work - the requirements, the problem domain and the technology - than it could. So it makes sense to delay breakdown, but delaying breakdown and estimation means there is little or no information about future work and the size of that work.

My solution here is *ballpark* estimates, to use an American expression. Call them *rough estimates* or *high-level* estimates if you prefer. These are estimates placed directly onto blue cards without any attempt at breakdown. They are intended as a guide and not as any form of commitment or guarantee. These estimates allow for some degree of forward planning.

Ballpark estimates are usually made on blues towards the end of the planning meeting. When the team has finished breaking down blues to whites, and when the work for the next iteration has been agreed, and if time allows, then the team may undertake some longer-range estimates.

Once all the work is decided, the Product Owner (PO) may present some blue cards for ballpark estimation. These may be cards that have recently been added to the backlog, or ideas that have been suggested recently. Or they may be existing blues the PO is considering for a future iteration. Discussion is kept general, specifics are, as far as possible, ignored, and generally these estimates are significantly larger numbers than those found on whites.

It is vital to remember that blue ballpark estimates are exactly that: estimates. They are for guidance only. Ballparks are not commitments, they are not accurate, and they are not specific. They are subject to change and bind nobody.

When the time comes for the blue to be developed, it will be broken down and the associated whites estimated exactly as above. The sum of these task estimates supersedes any ballpark estimate. The sum might be larger or smaller than the ballpark estimate. Indeed, if the sum of the tasks is regularly the same as the ballpark estimates then something is probably wrong and deserves more investigation.

5.2 Pre-Planning Meeting

Some teams move some of the activities to a pre-planning meeting, or in the case of a demo and retrospective, even a post-planning meeting. The difficulty with holding any meeting after the planning meeting is that any action arising can't be included in the iteration until the next planning meeting. For some teams this is acceptable, but in general most teams avoid the problem by holding these meetings before the planning meeting.

Since all pre-planning meeting activities eat into the time available during an iteration, to actually do work it is preferable to avoid them. However pre-planning can sometimes be useful.

Software demos are frequently held before the formal planning meeting. However, as the planning meeting represents the end of one iteration and the start of the next, holding the demo before the planning meetings creates a gap. During this gap the team might continue working on the software, in which case the demo is not complete. More worryingly, the software might get broken in this gap. Neither issue need be too problematic provided the demo is not held too far in advance.

A pre-planning meeting is usually an opportunity for the PO to flag up some of the stories they plan to request and get the team's feedback before the formal planning meeting. Teams may even use the pre-planning meeting to make ballpark estimates on blues. As a result of the feedback the PO might rethink what they actually request in the planning meeting a few days later.

Again there is a danger that if the pre-planning meeting is held too far in advance, changes may render it pointless. A second danger is that teams do too much preparation work in the pre-planning meeting and this work is invalidated by the end of the iteration (e.g. they break down stories which are then de-prioritised).

5.3 Planning Poker

Readers who have played planning poker may care to skip this section. For those who have not come across planning poker a quick description is appropriate.

Planning poker can be played with a normal set of playing cards, but is more normally played with a specially printed set numbered with an approximately Fibonacci sequence in order to spread estimates out. I like to use a set numbered zero, half, 1, 2, 3, 5, 8, 13, 21, 40, 65, 100, infinity and question mark. The last two of these are used to flag up problems such as "That is truly massive" or "I don't even know where to start".

Many training and consulting firms get planning poker card sets printed to give away as marketing material. In addition, there are now applications for mobile phones that can be used too. I am not a fan of such applications, because I believe in keeping planning sessions both physical and interactive.

A team may make their own planning poker cards. To do this each team member should take several index cards (of any colour) and write the following sequence on the cards - one number per card: half, 0, 1, 2, 3, 5, 8, 13, 21, 40, 65, 100, '?' and, if they want one, infinity.

To estimate a piece of work, the team members place the task card in the centre - easily done when work is on physical card. If the team is unfamiliar with this card there may need to be some discussion about what the card means. For example, if this is a blue business card, the PO may describe what is wanted. If it is a white card then - hopefully - the card was written only a few minutes before as a collective team effort.

Ideally during this pre-estimation discussion team members will avoid saying "Oh it's easy" or "That should be a six". When the team is ready, they each select a card from their playing cards, e.g. a 5 card or an 8 card, and keep it hidden. Somebody, either the PO, Scrum master, senior developer or just a team member, gives some kind of lead-in (e.g. "3, 2, 1" or "Ready... Steady... Vote") and on cue all team members reveal their card.

If all the cards agree, e.g. everyone plays 3, then the estimate is accepted and recorded on the card. If the estimates do not agree, there needs to be a second round of voting. Before re-voting someone will give an argument for the highest estimate and someone else for the lowest estimate. Normally only two people need to speak, one person speaking for the high vote and one speaking for the low. Those who voted in between remain silent; any duplicate high (or low) voters don't need to speak.

Normally this argument is a short statement of position. There is seldom a need to engage in lengthy debate. After the two positions are given, the voting process can be repeated exactly as before. Hopefully on the second vote the estimates are all in agreement. However this is seldom the case. At this point different teams do different things.

After a second vote some teams will engage in a negotiation. They would ask the lowest voters what it would take for them to go up and ask highest voters what it would take for them to go down. Some teams I have heard of will again state positions and play a third and even more rounds until convergence is achieved.

I advise teams to go with the majority vote (e.g. if four developers vote 8 and one votes 3 I would accept 8, in effect going with the median) or I would go with an approximate mean average (e.g. 7). At this point I am not concerned about the Fibonacci series; it has served its purpose, and to keep things moving fast I use all numbers. However some teams stick with the series and will not take numbers not on the cards.

Once one story or task card is estimated, attention shifts to the next. The intention is to keep estimation moving forward in order to estimate a lot of work quickly.

It is important to remember that these estimates are just that - estimates. The objective of planning poker is to be roughly right rather than precisely wrong. Coupled with velocity measures and rolling averages, accuracy is gained through metrics (averages and aggregates) over multiple estimates and work items, not through individually accurate estimates.

Baseline - what is 'one'?

Both new teams and existing teams adopting planning poker face one troublesome problem: what is 'one'?

In order to find a baseline, teams should take one blue that has been broken down into multiple white tasks. They should examine the whites and find the one which looks like the least effort. This process doesn't need to be exact or have complete agreement. This task then becomes *one*. One point, that is.

The team then take the next task, possibly the one that looked like the second least effort, or perhaps another. They play planning poker on this and obtain an effort value. The team now has two reference points and can continue.

When a team starts playing planning poker the value of 'one' is very variable. At first the team might feel a need to refer back to the baseline 'one'. Over time the team will gain an intrinsic understanding of what one point is, the value will become more stable and reference back to the baseline should cease. As the team actually do the work this understanding solidifies.

Over time the value of one point will change: the currency floats. This is perfectly acceptable. To draw an analogy: when someone goes to live in another country which uses another currency, they regularly calculate back to their home country's currency and prices. This works, but the same products cost different amounts in different currencies.

When I left the UK for the USA in 2000 the exchange rate was about £1 to $1.50. A gallon of gas (petrol) cost about $1.80 - a little over £1.20. This was high by US standards at the time, but unbelievably cheap by UK standards. To complicate matters, the UK sold petrol by litres, not gallons, and in a final twist a US gallon was about 3.7 litres and a UK gallon about 4.5 litres.

After a few weeks the expatriate stops translating back and starts to think in the new currency and reference local prices. (Holidays are seldom long enough to fully demonstrate this effect.)

Teams that stay together continue to use the same baseline as they move from story to story, iteration to iteration and even project to project. The value (in time) of one (unit of effort) changes, but it is good enough for short (one iteration) and medium (up to one quarter) range planning. Only if a team's membership changes significantly does it need to rebase 'one'.

Finally, as a team decides what one point is, and decides what two, five, 13 and others are, the team takes these values as shared values. Occasionally individuals try to use their own value system, even in parallel.

5.4 Some Planning Poker theory

The theory underpinning planning poker is 'Wideband Delphi' (see http://en.wikipedia.org/wiki/Wide_band_delphi for more about the history of this method.) You don't need to know that to play planning poker, but it does help to know a little of why this silly looking technique is useful:

- A psychological phenomenon known as 'anchoring' leads people to rely on the first piece of information that receives more than others. Coupled with social pressure to confirm, this means that "Oh that is easy, that should be 4 hours" people are likely to cluster their estimates around this statement, thus reducing the effectiveness of multiple independent estimates.
- It has been shown that experts are no better at giving time estimates than non-experts. What does improve estimation is having multiple independent estimates. (See Makridakis, Hogarth, and Gaba 2010; and Surowiecki 2004).

- Some other studies (e.g. Weick and Guinote 2010) report that the greater an individual's power and authority, the more optimistic their estimates. Thus we might expect a project manager or architect to provide lower estimates than junior developers.
- According to some researchers, humans produce better estimates when they estimate on behalf of others (Buehler, Griffin, and Ross 1994). Rather than ask "How long do you think it will take to do X?", we should ask "How long do you think it will take another team member to do X?".

The *planning fallacy* (Kahneman and Tversky 1979) also suggests that humans are more confident in their predictions than is warranted, and cling to beliefs even in the face of evidence of past under-estimation. Using planning poker and benchmarking against past performance (velocity) enables Xanpan to bring an element of predictability to the estimation process.

5.5 Why break down Blues?

I always advise teams to break down blue business-facing cards into white tasks. Although I often call whites 'developer tasks', this is slightly misleading, because they could be tasks for testers, analysts or anyone else. Breaking cards down has several benefits.

Stand-alone blue cards should have business value themselves, and they should also be small enough to be doable in the near future, e.g. within this iteration. These two aims can be in conflict: something which has stand-alone business value needs to be bigger, which means it cannot be accomplished soon. Breaking it down thus serves two purposes: it provides another opportunity to find small nuggets of business value, and provides a way of tracking progress on large pieces of work.

Breaking cards down also serves as a requirements elicitation process. Teams need to discuss the blue between themselves and with the Product Owner - this is why I like the PO to be in the room during this process. This dialogue serves to flush out details, additional requirements, assumptions and misunderstandings.

The breakdown is also a *design activity* because it causes the team members to discuss how they will approach the coding of the story. For some teams this design activity is a major part of the breakdown, while for others it is trivial.

Taken together the design and requirements elicitation serve to build a *shared understanding* between all team members: coders, testers and product people. In doing so it helps identify the key value elements of the stories and provides a forum for trade-offs to be made.

By breaking blue stories separately before estimating whites, a team engages in planning the tasks free from estimation. When estimation happens it is based on a scenario - the whites. This forces people to think about what is involved in achieving the goal, rather than the goal itself (Buehler, Griffin, and Ross 1994; Wiseman 2009). Part of the reason for optimistic estimates is that people focus on the goal, and the desirability of achieving the goal leads to wishful thinking.

Indeed, Wiseman advises that in setting a goal one should share it with friends and family, break the goal down into a series of sub-tasks, and reward oneself as you progress. This advice aligns with the process described here: blues are selected and publicly stated, they are broken down collectively to sub-tasks, and as each sub-task is completed it is moved across the board and the points scored. Because the breakdown is collective, it is open and shared: moving completed cards across the board is a public statement of success.

While blue business cards are normally written in user story format (As a... I can... So that...), the same is not true of whites. These are written in whatever language and format makes sense to the team. Similarly, while blues will typically have some acceptance criteria associated with them, whites do not. It is up to a developer to set their own criteria for whites, usually using unit testing.

(Because each blue represents business functionality, they may be tested by professional testers individually. Whites are not usually testable alone by professional testers.)

If in breaking cards down the Product Owner sees a white that they deem to have business value in and of itself, they may 'upgrade' the card to a blue. If this card then needs breaking down itself, it is broken down exactly the same way.

Some teams find they do not need to break down blues: the blues are themselves small enough to be worked on. This is perfectly acceptable. Similarly, some teams find that with experience they can dispense with the breakdown to whites. Generally I tend to find such teams work with more modern technologies, e.g. they are building websites in PHP or Ruby. Teams which benefit more from breakdown are working with older technologies or are further from the user, e.g. telecom and server systems written in C++ or Java.

5.6 Estimate in Points Not Hours

I always advise teams to estimate in points, not hours. I usually use the term *abstract points*, although some people called these *story points* (Cohn 2004) and several other terms are used, e.g. 'nebulous units of time'. The important point is: points are not hours. A point is an *unit of effort* - it is not, specifically, the amount of time it will take to do something, nor is it a measure of complexity. It is the measure of the effort required.

Some people estimate stories (blues) in some kind of points, but switch to hours for tasks. I do not recommend this approach. As I will describe in a moment, I don't believe humans can accurately estimate in hours. Secondly, I see little point in using one unit of measurement for stories and another for tasks. To my mind points are a team's currency, and using two different units is equivalent to having two currencies in circulation.

That said, I expect estimates on white tasks to be smaller than estimates on blue stories. When playing planning poker I expect whites to be estimated using the smaller numbers (1, 2, 5, etc.) and ballpark blue estimates to use the bigger numbers (21, 40, 65).

Occasionally I run across teams who estimate even the smallest items - tasks or stories - in larger numbers. Such teams' smallest estimate may be 10 points, and 100-point cards may be common. As long as the team benchmark against themselves, this doesn't matter. These teams have light currencies, akin to the old lira or drachma, while most teams have heavy currencies akin to the pound or dollar. The numbers themselves don't matter: what is important is what the currency will buy.

In 1979 two Pentagon researchers published a paper describing 'The Planning Fallacy' (Kahneman and Tversky 1979) - the same authors went on to win the Nobel prize for Economics for not entirely unrelated other work. The planning fallacy states:

- People tend to underestimate the amount of time that work will take to get done. This isn't occasional or random - it's systematic.
- People are overconfident in their own predictions, even when shown evidence of past optimism.

These findings have been upheld by multiple subsequent studies, (e.g. Zackay and Block 2004; Buehler, Griffin, and Ross 1994). The Zachay study is particularly interesting, in that it extends the 'planning fallacy' to *retrospective estimates*, i.e., asked to state how long it took to undertake a task they have already done, an individual will still make an underestimate of the time spent. Other studies (e.g. Buehler, Griffin, and Peetz 2010a) support the finding that the past is remembered optimistically.

Around the same time Douglas Hofstadter coined Hofstadter's Law:

'It always takes longer than you expect, even when you take into account Hofstadter's Law.' (Hofstadter 1980)

Hofstadter's Law is itself a reincarnation of Vierordt's law, which states that, retrospectively, 'short' intervals of time tend to be overestimated, and 'long' intervals of time tend to be underestimated. (See http://en.wikipedia.org/wiki/Vierordt%27s_law for a description of Vierordt's Law.)

When asked to estimate in hours a number of additional forces come into play: nobody wants to be considered a slacker at work; people may actively want to disguise how much time they spend doing a task; or they may consciously change their estimates in an effort to be assigned, or to avoid, a particular piece of work.

But estimating in points is only half the story: to complete the story, we need to consider the past performance of the team, their *velocity*. Only when both are known can accurate time-based estimates be made.

The primary reason for moving teams away from hours as an estimation unit is to help compensate for the planning fallacy. Estimating in points and comparing the points to past performance uses historical data, which individuals do not.

5.7 Ideal hours

Some teams prefer to estimate in 'ideal hours'. Unfortunately an ideal hour rarely exists, but using this expression itself creates misunderstanding. To team members it is some abstract measurement unit that vaguely resembles an hour; an ideal hour is an hour where everything went well: no interruptions, no distractions, no unexpected surprises.

To those outside the team it is an hour: 60 minutes of paid time.

The question is: when planning work, what does a team benchmark itself against?

If a team benchmarks itself on a standard 40-hour work week, then ideal hours need to add up to 40. If it does not, then management may well wonder what the team is doing with the rest of its contracted hours.

If instead the team benchmark against its past performance, then the unit of measurement is floating and is effectively an abstract point - by whatever name we choose to call it.

5.8 And 'Actuals'

Humans underestimate how long it takes to do a piece work, even in retrospect. Thus the thing that many companies call 'actuals', i.e. how long it took to actually undertake a piece of work, is nothing more than another estimate. A more realistic term for 'actuals' would be 'retrospective estimates'.

These retrospective estimates are generated by an individual rather than a team. These estimates do not benefit from multiple independent estimates used in prospective estimates. Retrospective estimates are the product of one person, and may reflect biases in the way they work - or how often they go the toilet.

Thus prospective and retrospective estimates are different currencies. Mixing the two is like mixing apples and oranges, or expecting to pay a $100 bill with $50 and £50.

Individuals could obtain more accurate 'actuals' by engaging in proactive time measurement, perhaps logging their activity every 15 minutes. The problem here is that such logging interferes with doing the work itself. At least one study I saw suggested - the actual results were inconclusive - that in keeping an accurate time record reduced people's their capacity to do work.

Because 'actuals' are so subjective, they can easily become the subject of much debate. Such debate is itself of little value, but causes animosity and wastes time.

At one company I met project managers who advised individuals on how much time to log against their assigned projects in order to keep 'actuals' in line with estimates. The managers were actively gaming the system to minimise variance between estimates and actuals, perhaps because their individual bonus was linked to this variance.

Consequently I ignore 'actuals'.

The time-tracking systems used by many corporations compound the problems with actuals. One friend of mine reports that the American bank he worked for did not allow more than the contracted 37 hours a week to be entered. And Capers Jones points out that few systems allow 'slack time' or unpaid overtime to be entered (Jones 2008). Jones reports that normal software measurement practices seldom collect more than 80% of the true effort. Jones also states that for MIS projects 60% the total effort can be lost.

As a consequence traditional time-tracking systems can be a major source of project risk. If time-tracking data from one development initiative is used to forecast and plan a new one, then the new work may immediately start with a 20% schedule slippage, and possibly a 20% budget overrun, simply because the benchmark was inaccurate.

While I would like teams to shun traditional time-tracking systems altogether, this may not be very acceptable in some environments. I advise people in this situation to double-think.

For work planning and estimation, use points and the tools described here. For filling in time-tracking systems, forget all that and use whatever mechanism you like. Such systems exist for the benefit of corporate accounting and have nothing to do with sizing work.

The golden rule is: do not let the data from the time-tracking system be used for planning purposes. These are two different currencies. Again, using them together would be like offering to pay a restaurant bill for $70 with a $20 bill and a £50 note.

5.9 Deadlines

The research mentioned above also throws up another interesting finding: people are very good at working to deadlines. In one study (Buehler, Griffin, and Ross 1994) the (external) deadline was met 80% of the time. This finding had nothing to do with estimates; estimates were still too low, but it seems people meet deadlines.

When I explain this to people I often ask a group "How many of you did courses at school or college which involved doing an assignment to be handed in to a deadline set by the teacher?". This is a familiar experience for most people. I then ask "When did you do it? How many of you did the work in plenty of time? And how many left it to the day or night before?". Overwhelmingly, most people leave assignments until as late as possible.

However leaving work until the last possible moment is itself a rational approach. Firstly it minimises the chances that work will go away or be changed. Secondly it allows one to maximise the learning time available before engaging in work. In fact it would be irrational to begin school assignments early, because it would deprive the student of knowledge the teacher will share.

When estimates are made with an externally imposed deadline, people change their estimating behaviour. In one experiment the researchers above set two groups the same task but with different deadlines. The ones with the later deadline provided larger estimates. Yet the extra time did not make a difference to the actual time taken to complete the task.

While subjects in the experiment denied letting the deadline influence their estimates, the estimates were highly correlated with the deadline. Possibly deadlines are imposing a form of anchoring; however, they are deadlines that can achieved.

Imposing deadlines - external deadlines - can be demotivating. In my own experience, when I have had an arbitrary deadline imposed on me at work, I am demotivated.

However, this anecdote does not seem to stand up to research. It seems that externally imposed deadlines are more effective at delivering task completion (Buehler, Griffin, and Peetz 2010b), and regular evenly spaced deadlines are more effective still (Ariely and Wertenbroch 2002).

The planning process described here exploits these factors in several ways:

- Estimates are kept free from deadlines.
- Deadlines are effective when externally imposed and occur regularly.
- Fairness is maintained, because team members decide between themselves what they will do in the time, and,

over the longer term, have a say in how regularly the deadline happens.

- If a customer wants a piece of work by a particular date (and I encourage them to think like this), then there is a negotiation with the development team over what can be achieved in the time.

5.10 References

Ariely, D., and K. Wertenbroch. 2002. "Procrastination, deadlines, and performance: self-control by precommitment." *Psychological Science* 13 (3).

Buehler, R., D. Griffin, and J. Peetz. 2010a. "The Planning Fallacy: Cognitive, Motivational, and Social Origins." *Advances in Experimental Social Psychology* 43: 1–62.

———. 2010b. "Finishing on time: When do predictions influence completion times?" *Organizational Behavior and Human Decision Processes* (111).

Buehler, R., D. Griffin, and M. Ross. 1994. "Exploring the 'Planning Fallacy:' Why People Underestimate Their Task Completion Times." *Journal of Personalty and Social Psychology* 67 (3): 366–381.

Cohn, M. 2004. *User Stories Applied.* Addison-Wesley.

Hofstadter, Douglas R. 1980. *Godel Escher Bach: An eternal golden braid.* Harmondsworth: Penguin Books.

Jones, C. 2008. *Applied Software Measurement.* McGraw Hill.

Kahneman, and Tversky. 1979. "Intuitive Prediction: Biases and Corrective Procedures." *TIMS Studies in Management Science* (12): 313–327.

Makridakis, S., R. M. Hogarth, and A. Gaba. 2010. "Why Forecasts Fail. What to Do Instead." *MIT Sloan Management Review* 51 (2).

Surowiecki, James. 2004. *The wisdom of crowds*. 1st ed.. New York: Doubleday. http://www.loc.gov/catdir/bios/random055/2003070095.html.

Weick, M., and A. Guinote. 2010. "How long will it take? Power biases time predictions." *Journal of Experimental Social Psychology* 46.

Wiseman, R. 2009. *59 Secods*. Macmillan.

Zackay, D., and R. A. Block. 2004. "Prospective and retrospective duration judgments: an executive-control perspective." *Acta Neurobiol Ex* (64): 319–328.

6 Watching the numbers

The team described in Board 1 were very good at watching their numbers. 'Watching' being the operative word; as I will discuss later, targeting numbers can lead to all sorts of undesirable behaviour.

6.1 Where does the time go?

Xanpan teams commonly have more than one work stream (product, project, unplanned or other work) in play at one time. Whatever the work, it is recorded on the board as either planned or unplanned work. This allows the team to analyse where the time goes and to adjust accordingly.

For example, an iteration scoring 28 points might find the following breakdown:

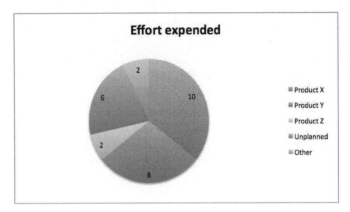

Effort pie chart

Given this breakdown, the team might decide to take action to reduce unplanned work or understand what 'other' work is and how it might be reduced. In the case of the previous team the unplanned work was mainly IT support, and after a while they hired an IT support engineer to handle it.

It can also be interesting to compare multiple iterations to see what patterns emerge, as shown in the following figure.

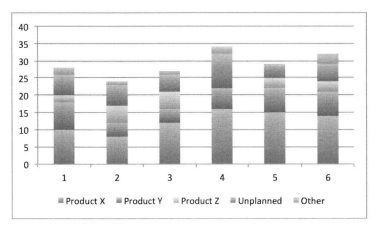

Effort over iterations

At a very basic level a team will want to track the total effort, usually called *velocity*, that they achieve each week, and again this should be tracked.

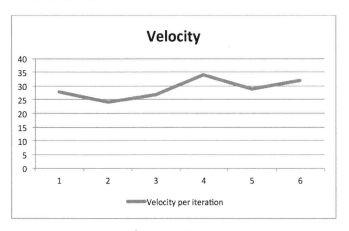

Velocity per iteration

However, what might be more useful for planning purposes is to track the velocity per product, as shown in the next diagram.

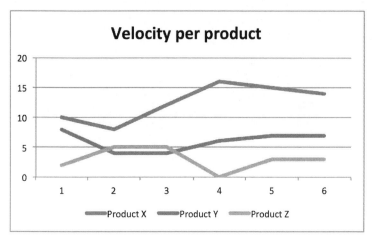

Velocity per product

This allows a number of 'what if' games to be played, such as "What if we suspended all work on Product X to put all effort into Product Y?". Combined with planning and estimating techniques discussed here and later, this can allow for accurate forecasts.

6.2 Hitting a deadline

One of the keys to success for the Falmouth team described before was the attention paid to metrics. For example, the manager concerned tracked (in points) where the team's effort went: how many points to each in-flight project, how many points on unplanned work, how many points on support and so on. He kept graphs (shown in the pictures) of where the effort went, and worked to eliminate non-value adding areas and focus the team more tightly on core projects.

As a result of tracking the numbers, he was able to calculate a multiplier linking initial story estimates (the ballpark estimates on blue cards) with the final number of points expended on a project. This multiplier changes, but at one point it was 2.3.

Let's do a worked example: assume the team was given a new project for which someone had written a brief or requirements document (the nature of the start changed over time). The team would initially sit down and write blue story cards for the work they thought needed doing. Each one of these would be estimated - probably using planning poker - and a total effort level calculated. Call this the *initial effort estimate.*

During the course of the project more work would be added ('scope creep' if you want to call it that, but 'dark matter' is another name). Some work would go away. Some of the ballpark estimates would be high and some low. As each blue was broken down to whites and the whites estimated, the ballpark estimate would be replaced by the sum total of all the whites, which is generally regarded as a more detailed estimate. While this could in theory be higher or lower than the ballpark estimate, it is more likely than not to be higher.

At the end of the project all the effort estimates on all the completed (white) cards could be added together to calculate the *final effort.* Final effort would inevitably be different from the initial effort estimate. Now a multiplier, call it M, can be calculated so that:

Final effort = M x Initial effort estimate

For example, assume the initial effort estimate from the sum of the blue cards was 152, and the final effort (from all the completed whites) was 349. Then

$$349 = M \times 152$$

$$M = 349 / 152 = 2.3$$

With several completed projects providing several data sets this multiplier could be averaged. At one time this was M=2.3. (The multiplier may also be determined from comparing the initial estimates on blue cards with the final total of whites associated with the blue when it is complete.)

Given this the answer to the question "When will it be ready?" would be:

$$\text{Weeks from today} = (I \times M) / A \times W$$

Where:

I = Sum total initial effort estimate

M = historical effort multiplier

A = Average recent velocity per iteration (e.g. over last 4 iterations)

W = Number of weeks per iteration

Perhaps replacing 'average recent velocity per iteration' with something which acknowledges that the team cannot put all their effort into one work stream would be more realistic, such as 'average velocity realised per iteration on previous work'.

Thus, if the initial effort estimate is 200 points, expect velocity is 12 points per iteration, the multiplier 2.3 and each iteration 2 weeks, the calculation becomes:

$$\text{Weeks from today} = ((200 \times 2.3) / 12) \times 2 = 75 \text{ weeks}$$

The manager in charge of this team once said: "This isn't estimation - that is Mystic Meg Stuff, this is science" and "We can bring a project in to the day."

Importantly, in order for the metrics to maintain their efficacy they must be allowed to change. The multiplier and average velocity need to be recalculated on a regular basis. Only by using relevant, recent, historical data can these calculations have any validity.

As convincing as the mathematics may seem, I believe there was a bit more to it than this. Yes the mathematics were sound, but there were psychological effects at work too. Given a realistic and believable delivery date, the team and its stakeholders could add and remove stories and increase and reduce the scope of the stories in the backlog. In other words, given an agreed deadline, the work was managed to meet the deadline. Over time the 2.3 multiplier would become a self-fulfilling forecast.

The obvious question that arises here is: could the team actively change the multiplier? I believe not, because to do so would turn an observed statistical regularity into a control parameter. According to Goodhart's Law, this would then cause the correlation to collapse. (I will discuss Goodhart's Law and its far-reaching implications later.)

Arguably there is also a placebo effect at work. Despite the possibly jovial nature of planning poker and weirdness of not estimating in units of time the team had a rational process and the mathematics added to the rationality of it all. The team and the wider company came to believe the process. The team felt committed to their own estimates and the company felt they could trust the team. It created an environment where scope and dates could be discussed.

Even if there were no benefits to the estimation process - and I believe there were - it would still be worth doing to create the environment. However, like the Emperor's new clothes, examining the process too closely might remove credibility and render it useless.

Finally here a word of warning. As convincing as the above calculation and discussion is I would strongly avoid projecting beyond the next 12 weeks, i.e. 3 months or one-quarter - as discussed in the *Planning beyond the Iteration* chapter. Velocity changes, any projection based on a changing variable is unreliable. Secondly long range projection risks invoking Goodhart's Law in respect of velocity; when velocity is used in this fashion it becomes a target which will change.

Deadlines should be met by being flexible about what is build rather than projecting estimates forward. Be prepared to change the thing being build in order to meet the deadline.

6.3 Other numbers

Velocity and the estimation multiplier are far from the only metrics I expect a team to track. They are important, and I would hope a team would track them as described here. However they are only one example of a metric that can be tracked.

Each team will be different; the metrics that a team should and will track will differ from team to team. Some of the metrics I would expect a team to track are as follows:

- Size of the product backlog: measured in points or simply a card count.
- The rate of change of the backlog. Is it growing? Shrinking? If so, what is the monthly average?
- The rate of change of backlog change. Is the backlog growing (or shrinking) faster than previously?
- The outstanding (open) defect count. To paraphrase a more famous speaker, "Two bugs are a tragedy, 2000 bugs are a statistic". Is the bug count growing or falling? Is the rate of discovering increasing or decreasing? And why?
- Working hours: are people working more than their contracted hours? And who is paying for this? How long has it been going on for? Is it reducing overall capacity?
- Effort per work stream: where is the time going, and is it where the effort is wanted?
- Mean time to delivery: what is the average time a feature request spends waiting in the backlog before it is developed? And once it enters development, how long does it typically spend in development?

- Mean time to fix: as before, what is the average time between defect report and defect fix?

Advanced statisticians should also be looking at distribution data: how stable is velocity? Is velocity normally distributed? Is work arriving according to normal distribution, Poisson, or some other distribution?

Given this data, what forecasts can be made?

Most of these statistics concern the input and cost side of the equation. It might be more difficult still to assess benefits, but those too should be tracked:

- Revenue derived from new products and features in the last quarter.
- Deals signed as a result of new functionality, defect fixes, or other recent development.
- Change in costs on support desks.
- Business disruption (better or worse) from IT activities/lack of activity.

In measuring all these numbers, bear in mind the economist's maxim "Do not read too much into one set of figures." But also bear in mind the riposte "Never ignore one month's figures."

In other words: it is the trend that is important, and trends only become apparent over time. Unfortunately that also means they occur in retrospect, by which time it might be too late - the damage may be done.

Therefore, capture metrics over time, look for trends and act on them. But when an anomaly occurs, investigate. Before excusing it as a 'one off', at least seek to understand why it happened, at least consider the possibility that this is the point at which a new trend emerges.

And if it is a trend you do not want, then act.

Key points

- Track the numbers: use the numbers to understand, don't make targets of observations.
- Graph the numbers to understand where effort is going.
- Seek out relationships such as estimated versus final points to completion.
- Recognise that there are other factors at work.
- Track planned and unplanned work.
- Recognise different work streams, know when to combine and when to separate.

7 Board 2

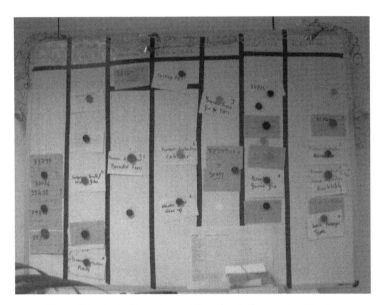

Figure 7.1 - Actual board providing for daily re-prioritisation

Aficionados of board design will immediately recognise this board to be decidedly more Kanban in style than traditional Scrum boards. The next illustration shows the key elements of this board more clearly.

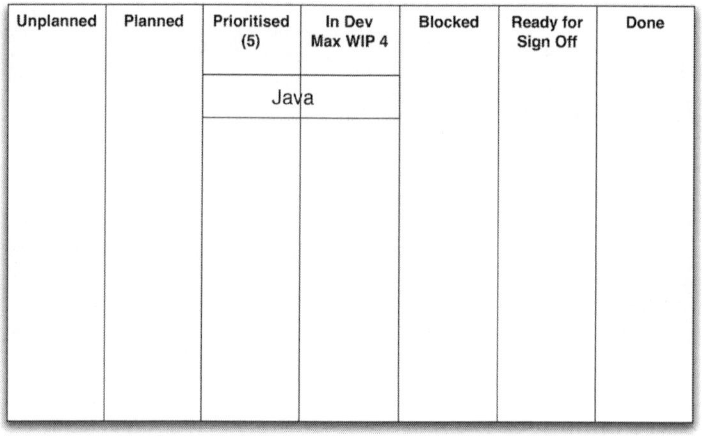

Unplanned	Planned	Prioritised (5)	In Dev Max WIP 4	Blocked	Ready for Sign Off	Done
			Java			

Figure 7.2 - Simplified board for daily re-prioritisation

The board shown in these two figures was used by a team which regularly had unplanned work inserted into the iteration after it started but was still expected by management to deliver a 'project'. This team adopted a different strategy to the first team.

('Project' for this team was a particular misnomer. The team originally came with the purchase of another company, and while the rest of the company worked in Java, they worked mostly in C. The team continued from one project to another, but the code base, the team and the type of work remained the same.)

7.1 Planned and Unplanned

This team adopted 3-week iterations - my least favourite length. Every three weeks the team met to review the work completed and schedule more work. The chosen work (Sprint backlog) was placed on the board in the Planned column and the iteration would start.

Almost every day new requests would be made of the team. While most of these would be bug fixes on a live system, others would be unforeseen but urgent requests for change. These would be put on index cards - probably not in user story format. Since most of these items would be bugs, they would be put on red cards and placed in the unplanned column - most unplanned work was bugs.

Every morning, a few minutes before the daily stand-up meeting, the team leader and the product manager would gather at the board and review:

- The unplanned work that had arisen since the start of the iteration (in the Unplanned column).
- The planned work that had not yet entered development (in the Planned column).
- Work resting in the Prioritised column.

From these three columns they would determine the day's priorities, which would then populate the Prioritised column. When a team member became available they would choose their next task from the Prioritised column.

The team had also imposed a work in progress limit of five (more of these later) on the Development column (there were five developers on the team) so it didn't make much sense for a lot more than five items to be prioritised that day. In the event that the Prioritised column ever did empty during the day, the product manager and/or team leader would simply pull another card, or cards, from the Planned or Unplanned column.

Once a card had entered the Prioritised column it was likely to stay there until moving into development. Occasionally a card might make it to Prioritised only to find that before work actually commenced it was de-prioritised back to the Planned or Unplanned column from where it came.

Cards would be marked to show whether they entered as Planned or Unplanned work. A count could then be made on the cards which reached 'done' to understand the nature of the work the team was undertaking.

This team also utilised a blocked area on the board. In this case the blocked area was a vertical column. If a card was never blocked, it would simply jump over this column. I don't think I've used a vertical blocked column since this time and I wouldn't recommend it. Having part of one or more columns partitioned off at the bottom works much better.

7.2 Testers

As with the previous team discussed, this team did not contain any dedicated test resource, so the developers themselves undertook all testing. Unlike the previous team, this company did employ testers, albeit in a different team and in a different time zone. When these testers found a problem with the software, the problem entered the system as a red card in the Unplanned column. Unfortunately the testers lagged several weeks or even months behind the developers, so their feedback was seldom timely.

Although they had no testers, the developers would wherever possible show their work to the product manager before setting it to 'done'. Hence, when a developer completed a card, they would move it from In Development to Ready For Sign-off. The product manager would periodically review the cards in Ready for Sign-off - with the Developer if appropriate - and then move it to 'done'. If they did not accept the card, it would move back to one of the first three columns.

7.3 Moving backwards

Cards shouldn't move backwards across the board, i.e. from right to left. However, it happens. That a card needs to move backwards is a sign of a problem. Moving a card backwards - that is, accepting that it has been allowed to advance too far and pushing it back - is the least disruptive option.

One alternative would be to ignore the problem. This isn't a good option, because it relies on luck, equivalent to crossing one's fingers and hoping the observed problem doesn't cause problems later on.

Another option is to let the card remain in the current position - or even let it progress forward - but to raise a red card to ensure a fix is applied. This creates the illusion that work is done, and might be accepted for release, when it is not. It also raise the prospect that the red fix might be pulled itself, or delayed, thereby allowing an actual problem into production.

In some teams raising a red would even involve raising a formal bug in a tracking system. This creates an administration over-head, and can sometimes deter people from raising the problem in the first place.

The least bad solution is simply to move the original card back. The long-term solution is to put in place mechanisms to prevent such problems in the first place.

7.4 Planning

When the iteration finished the team would review the board and clear down the 'done' cards. This team was not estimating cards in terms of points, but instead simply marking them 'small', 'medium' or 'large' - so called 'T-shirt sizing'. These sizings were used purely to help the product manager and project manager in setting the day's priorities. There was no velocity measurement or forecasting.

The team tracked the dates the card moved between columns on the back of each card. This allowed them to monitor the time it took for a card to move from 'prioritised' to 'done'. Over time this could be averaged out to provide - for each size of card - the expected turn-around time once a card had reached 'prioritised'. Of course, simply getting to 'prioritised' could take a while.

In the planning meeting, the very start of the iteration, there should be no unplanned work. Any unplanned work carried over becomes planned by virtue of having been reviewed in the planning meeting. The point of the planning meeting is that it plans known work. So regardless of whether a piece of work originated months ago and has sat in a backlog all this time, or suddenly appeared from nowhere two days ago, it becomes planned. Thus any work in the Unplanned column at the start of the planning meeting would be planned by the end of it.

That said, what was important to the team was monitoring and tracking work that appeared randomly - and urgently - and the work that could be scheduled. Therefore unplanned work was either de-scoped or left where it was in the Unplanned column. The source of work was more important than the exact timing of arrival.

7.5 Specialists

One less than perfect feature of this board is the special Java area. Small sections, just big enough to comfortably hold one card, have been sectioned off on both the Prioritised and In Progress columns. Although there were five developers in the team, four of them worked in C.

The C developers originally came from the purchased company, understood the system in detail and formed quite a close-knit group. While some of these developers had more knowledge of some parts of the system than others they could all, in general, pick up any cards that involved C work. This greatly simplified scheduling, as the next developer to become available would pick up the next 'C' card.

The fifth developer only worked in Java and had joined the team after the acquisition; indeed he was quite new to the company. The Java developer had no desire to learn or work in C, and the C developers felt little compulsion to work in Java, although they had been told that they would need to eventually. Fortunately the bulk of the code was in C - the Java code largely related to the interface with the rest of the company.

This situation was clearly less than perfect - and counter to the ideas set out here about teams. However this was the situation as found, and was not going to change simply because it was inconvenient, so some coping mechanism was needed.

The solution was to identify which cards - of whatever colour - required work in Java by writing 'J'ï°½ on the card: by definition everything else was in C. The team leader and product manager always ensured there was one 'J' card waiting in the Prioritised column, and the developer would work on one card at a time.

Well, that was the original plan. A surprising number of J cards quickly became blocked. They moved from 'in progress' to 'blocked' and the developer pulled another card. When we inquired into what was happening, it turned out that the Java developer blocked because he didn't understand other aspects of the company system. He would send e-mails to people asking questions, and while he was waiting, move the cards to 'blocked'. Nobody else on the team was in a position to help him, and being relatively new to the company he knew little of the wider system or who was the right person to ask was.

Once the issue was identified, the team leader and product manager could help the Java developer find the answers to his questions. In some cases it was simply a matter of giving him the confidence to ask questions orally in person or on the telephone.

7.6 Technical Debt (and tax)

This team, indeed the whole company, had an accepted technical debt problem that had been highlighted all the way to board level. The company had decided this sub-system - a flight booking system - would not be rebuilt, but the team was authorised to spend time making technical improvements.

Some teams call this 'paying your taxes'. Rather than engineers and business representatives arguing over each and every possible technical improvement - something that usually leaves both sides feeling short-changed - a 'tax level' is decided at a strategic level, e.g. a 20% tax is accepted by management, who then allow engineers to nominate 20% of all work done.

(Developers often dislike the term 'tax' and prefer to use the term 'investment'. Indeed the tax is used for investing in the longevity and maintainability of the system so 'investment' may well be a better term. However this can be a complex conversation which distracts from actually setting the tax/investment level itself.)

The tax can be paid in several ways. For teams estimating and working in points, a tax level of 25% may mean that one quarter of the points for work in an iteration are nominated by development engineers rather than business representatives. The team then need to decide whether the 25% comes from the first ('guaranteed') points, or the last 25% ('if lucky') points.

Alternatively the same tax may be implemented by turning over every fourth iteration to the developers. No new functionality is developed during the iteration; indeed, the developers need to keep functionality and appearance unchanged. They are only allowed to change the insides.

(Developers are not allowed to use their tax time to work on features they wish the business would implement, but has not prioritised.)

For this team a tax level of 60% had been set, perhaps the highest level I have personally ever seen. This was implemented simply by having the product manager and project manager ensure that three out of five cards in the Prioritised column at any one time were improvement cards, and only two were enhancing business functionality.

At the end of the iteration we counted the improvement and business cards. Perhaps surprisingly the ratio of 'done' cards was two-thirds improvement, one third business. While technically that might imply a tax level of 66%, the difference was not a cause for worry. What was important was that we had a simple, effective and cheap to administer means of operating the tax level.

7.7 Key points

- The Planned, Unplanned and Prioritised columns were reviewed daily by those with authority to set priorities for the team.
- The team imposed work in progress limits.
- Work was provisionally reviewed before it was finally considered done.
- The team had an active tax policy for addressing technical debt.

8 Non-technical Practices

There are a number of practices that I regard as central to Xanpan. From the stories in this text, some of the practices should be clear. Teams may vary even these practices, but on the whole these are the practices which define a Xanpan team in action.

8.1 Work in routines

Iterations, stand-up meetings, reviews, retrospectives and other set-piece events should occur on regular schedules. These schedules create a rhythm to work, they impose deadlines and create a framework within which work happens.

Typical set-piece routines might be:

Event	Frequency
Iteration	Every 2 weeks - 10 working days
Stand-up meeting	Everyday - Maximum 15 minutes
Iteration review meeting	End of every iteration 20 minutes at end of iteration
Retrospective event	End of every iteration
Formal retrospective	End of every iteration (new teams);

Event	Frequency
(60-90 minutes)	every second (mature teams)
Informal retrospective (30mins)	Every second iteration for mature teams
Demo	At least every iteration which does not release
Release	Minimum quarterly - high-performing teams will release many times during iteration

8.2 Multiple work streams per team

In an ideal world one team would work on one work stream: call it a 'product' or call it a 'project', it's work. This would allow the team to focus just on this one thing. Above all else it keeps everything simple. It works, it works well, and it even happens occasionally. However, most of the teams I see have to deal with more than one work stream. They have multiple products to work on; some of this work goes by the name of 'projects', but not all, and some is plain old 'maintenance'.

Multiple work streams to one team can work and can work well. There are two keys to making it work effectively. Firstly, accept that it happens, and instead of managing around the product or project, take a team-centric view. It is the team, not the project, not even the product, which is the focus of activity.

Secondly, with the team at the centre of thinking it becomes a question of effectively supplying the team with work. The team does work: where the work comes from and how it is accounted for are almost irrelevant questions to the team members. The first job of management and leaders is to keep the team supplied with a valuable stream of work to do. Next one can consider how to optimise the team to work across streams, work to level the peaks and troughs in each stream, and avoid simultaneous peaks or troughs across multiple streams. Track metrics across multiple streams and learn to give reports and estimates in conditional terms: 'On current performance Project X will be finished, provided Project Y can be contained as we have been doing'.

8.3 Benchmark against yourself

Almost every financial product in the UK comes with a warning: 'Past performance is no indicator of future performance', or words to that effect. Unlike in financial services, in software development the case is reversed: 'Past performance is a good indicator of future performance'.

That statement comes with a caveat of its own: '...provided nothing significant changes'. Work out what constitutes 'significant' for your team. Common examples include people leaving the team, the team expanding at an inappropriate pace, work streams changing direction or being disrupted, other resources suddenly becoming unavailable, and so on.

This cuts both ways. If things aren't going well, then no amount of positive thinking and leader exhortation will make things go right. Unless you do something to fix the problems you are finding, they won't suddenly be fixed. Nor will they be fixed simply because you declare yourself to be doing Agile, Scrum, Xanpan or anything else. Equally, if things are going well, it is reasonable to expect them to continue to go well. Forecasts of future deliveries and schedules can be made with some degree of certainty - if you get the techniques right.

This all means that teams must examine and understand their past performance. Above all, it is the team's own past performance that counts and should be used as a benchmark - not some other team in the organisation, not some industry norm or a 'best in class' team. It is not even possible with any accuracy to have one team provide estimates for work another team will do.

To have any idea of how a team will perform in future, there must be a track record to look at. That means the team must have worked together before. That in turn makes it extremely difficult for a new team to make any forecasts. Indeed to do so is, in my book at least, close to professional malpractice.

8.4 Break down stories to tasks

As I outlined in the iteration planning meeting discussion, Xanpan teams break stories, in user story format or not, down into development tasks. Not every Agile team does that, and possibly advanced Xanpan teams wouldn't need to do so. However, in my experience having the team break down large items to individual tasks - ideally tasks that can each be achieved in one sitting - is an effective way of working, and can improve flow.

8.5 Small pieces of work

By imposing deadlines, and by breaking down the work, teams are constantly searching for small pieces of useful work. Small pieces of work flow through the delivery process more easily. However, getting to 'small' is hard. It takes teams time to learn how to get small. There are some techniques that can be adopted to help, and having a quality code base helps, but it does not happen instantly or by mandate.

The goal is ultimately to be able to size the work to the time available. Rather than asking "How long will it take to build X?", the discussion needs to be framed as "Given Y amount of time, how much of X can we build?" If X is composed of many independent, small, deliverable, valuable items, then this is a far easier question to answer.

Indeed, this practice was originally stated as "Size the work to fit the time available", which is what the team is aiming for. But day-to-day, especially when new to Agile and Xanpan, teams are actually practising a search for small work items.

8.6 Planning horizons

There are three rolling planning horizons in Xanpan:

- *Iteration plan*: looking two weeks into the future with a high degree of certainty about what is being worked on and delivered. This plan is primarily the concern of those building the product, mainly the programmers and testers.

- *Quarterly plan*: looking about 12 weeks, probably six iterations, into the future with limited certainty over what is being work on and delivered. This plan is primarily the concern of the requirements and specification group - Product Owners, managers and business analysts. Senior developers and architects may also have input here. The aim is a) to ensure work is prepared for the next iteration, and b) to allow coordination with other parts of the organisation
- *Roadmap*: starting at the end of the quarterly plan and looking years into the future. Team members and others in the wider organisation who are charged with strategic thinking will manage the roadmap. There is very little certainty in the roadmap, it is really a 'what if' discussion document.

These three horizons are covered in a later chapter.

8.7 Flow

By 'flow' I mean the movement of work through a system and the interactions involved - system, people, processes, things, work and so on. The idea is taken directly from Lean and Toyota. Flow can be optimised for different objectives. Common objectives are rapid throughput, lowest cost, predictability and consistency.

However, it is necessary to further quantify these objectives in each context. For example, a system that is optimised to achieve rapid throughput of all items may not be optimised for the fastest throughput of any one item. That is to say, a system designed to allow special work items to be 'expedited' may result in very rapid throughput for such items, but overall the average throughput time for most items may increase.

Predictability is another interesting case. Achieving predictability may mean some activities in the flow process are over-resourced, with either more people or more equipment than is absolutely essential. This of course drives up costs when measured per unit of activity, but may actually lower overall costs, because other activities in the system, or the system itself, performs better.

In optimising flow there are inevitably trade-offs like these to be made. Therefore optimising flow usually occurs within some constraints. Many Lean ideas such as production levelling, demand management, waste reduction, rework reduction, 'pull' and more are applicable in this context.

Work-in-progress limits, or just WIP limits, are a popular mechanism for improving flow. There are several ways in which WIP limits can be effected. Perhaps the most visible approach is placing numeric limits on columns on a board. These limits serve to restrict the number of items that may be in a column at any one time, i.e. the activity represented by the column is limited. The other way of implementing a WIP limit is by time rather by activity. In this case only so much work is allowed into the system over a period of time.

Xanpan utilises both forms of WIP limits, although some teams may only implement one.

Many teams do not initially set activity WIP limits. When they do, they are implemented by restricting the number of work items (cards) in a column on the board. Typically the WIP limit is set at one card per person. (Naturally this limit may be changed with the benefit of experience.)

Even if activity WIP limits are not placed explicitly, individuals are encouraged to only work on one item at a time. The assumption in both cases is that most individuals work predominantly on one activity, and their time is best used by focusing on one item until it is completed.

By placing activity WIP limits on some activities, several things happen. Firstly those working on the limited tasks improve their focus and should, hopefully, be able to get work done sooner. Secondly, and probably more importantly, by artificially restricting flow at some points, overall throughput can be improved. Rather than many items all moving through the system slowly, the artificial limits allow a few items to move through the system faster. (See (Goldratt and Cox 1993) for an explanation of this point and theory of constraints.)

Time-based WIP limits are implemented when loading the iteration (in the planning meeting) by the velocity and estimation system used in Xanpan. Teams only accept into the iteration a little more work than they expect to do. Other work is by definition not in progress, it is in some backlog somewhere.

Both types of limit allow the team to reason about the operation of the board, the system as a whole, and the interactions both within the system and outside it. Being able to see the limits and reason about the system present opportunities to improve the system as a whole.

Xanpan seeks to optimise flow over the wider system, where the optimisation goal is set externally to the system and may occasionally change. The definition of 'system' is likely to increase over time, but to start with 'system' may be defined narrowly. Because Xanpan is team-centric, the overall strategy is to 'flow the work to the team' and to optimise the team for predictable deliveries and increasing efficiency (leading to reduced time).

8.8 Mental flow

Before leaving the subject of flow, it is worth noting that 'flow' has another meaning, one not completely inconsistent with these ideas:

> 'Flow is the mental state of operation in which a person performing an activity is fully immersed in a feeling of energised focus, full involvement, and enjoyment in the process of the activity'. From Wikipedia, http://en.wikipedia.org/wiki/Flow_(psychology)

In optimising system flow, Xanpan aims to deliver mental flow, thus allowing each individual both to contribute to the full, and even to enjoy their work. This in turn should lead to even better work flow.

8.9 Absolute Prioritisation

Ideally I would like to see all possible work in priority order: 1, 2, 3, etc. with no duplicates. Certainly when it comes to scheduling work into an iteration it is essential that the team are told in no uncertain terms which is the highest priority work item and which is the least.

MoSCoW rules (Must, Should, Could and Won't/Would Like) might be useful as a first cut when faced with a large number (say more than 50) of items of work to do, but in most cases the majority of the items end up being classified as 'must'. Moscow is all right in the first instance, but the 'musts' need more attention.

Certainly if a business representative asks a team for several 'must-have' items and does not specify their priority order, they are passing final responsibility to the team. If the business genuinely does not care which item is delivered first and which last (or not at all if something happens in the meantime), then this is acceptable. However, business representatives often do care about what is delivered, and when. Therefore work should be priority ordered in no uncertain terms when agreed with the team. If all goes well the team should start work on the first item and work its way to the bottom. However there may be reasons why some items are skipped or done out of order. This is acceptable insomuch as there is a valid reason.

It does not matter what criteria are used to order the work. Some will argue for a business value-based approach, others for a risk-based approach. Tom Gilb has advocated a 'juicy bits first' ordering, and some organisations create complex formulae to balance several criteria. The criteria used are unimportant: what is important is that the priority ordering occurs and stays (mostly, usually) consistent for the length of the iteration.

Another technique that can replace Moscow rules is Tom Gilb's 'Single Sheet of A4' or 'Top 10' approach. Here a mass of requirements is reduced to either a Top 10 list or a single side of A4 paper. Again, once these summarised lists are produced, the items can simply be ordered from 1 to N, where N is the total number of items.

8.10 Product Ownership

Before any development can take place, some thought needs to be given to what is to be developed. It is easy to think of things one would like software to do - too easy, perhaps. These ideas need to be evaluated and filtered. And there are usually more good ideas than can be developed and delivered in the short term, so some form of prioritisation needs to take place.

While I have heard discard rates of 30% or 50% for backlog items, the context and validity of these figures are unclear. Certainly most product backlogs contain many items that do not stand up to serious analysis.

Those doing the work need to be given a clear guide on what the priorities are at any point in time - especially during planning meetings. They may also require protection from those in the organisation who would come directly to developers, circumventing any regular channels, and pull them in different directions, or those who practise 'decibel management' to get their own preferences developed.

Doing all the above, and more, is the practice of *product ownership*. This work is normally undertaken by a dedicated *Product Owner*, who is tasked with such work. The Product Owner is a fully fledged member of the development team.

The person undertaking product ownership probably has the job title and skills of business analyst, product manager or similar. They are specialists in 'requirements engineering' - indeed they may even have the title Requirements Engineer.

In Xanpan, unlike Scrum, product ownership is considered a practice rather than a role. This is because the work needs to be done whether there is a specialist filling the role or not. When there is no dedicated specialist, the work often falls to someone else. For example:

- *Project managers* often end up undertaking product ownership when no specialist is available. While their skill set is usually similar, they often tend to emphasis the 'when' rather than the 'what'.
- *Development managers* are another group who often end up undertaking product ownership. In my experience both the titles 'Project Manager' and 'Development Manager' are surprisingly elastic, and are often a catch-up title. Some development managers are in effect just project managers, others are mostly line/personnel managers. This makes it difficult to generalise about development managers.
- *Actual customers, subject matter experts* or *domain experts*: these roles correspond roughly to XP's 'Customer' role. Such people are experts in the existing technology, systems and processes. They can be an excellent choice when detailed knowledge of existing mechanisms are required but may, for the same reason, be less concerned with how things could be changed and with strategic thought.
- *Senior developers*: as with project and development managers, more senior developers often fill the void when no specialist is available. Again this can be a good stopgap; however it leads to the question: is this the best use of the developer's time?

If they are really good developers, should they be spending

their time on the requirements side - meeting customers and stakeholders? (And do they have the skills to do so?)

Conversely, if these individuals are really good at the requirement side, is coding an effective use of their time?

On a small piece of work, having a knowledgeable developer undertake requirements and product ownership can be highly successful, because it eliminates the need for any form of hand-over. However, once work grows, such individuals will naturally tend towards one side - analysis or synthesis - and the other side will be neglected.

This is by no means an exhaustive list. At a pinch almost anyone can undertake product ownership. The key thing, and the reason it is listed as a practice, is: no matter who does it, it needs doing. (Later chapters look at product ownership in more depth.)

8.11 Pick 'n Mix

As I described in the *Origins of Xanpan* chapter, Xanpan is a hybrid method built from pieces of other Agile processes and elsewhere. This philosophy should be baked into every team.

Agile is a label, 'waterfall' is a label, Scrum and Kanban are labels. Look beyond the label: what does that label describe? What practices? What processes? What principles? What tools? And what techniques?

Teams are encouraged to beg, borrow and steal from anywhere to build their own 'method'. This approach should be coupled with the next practice...

8.12 Action over words: 'just-do-it', experimentation

Finally, Xanpan emphasises a 'bias for action' - to use the words of management guru Tom Peters. There is an assumption that to understand the work, one must engage in doing the work.

This should breed a culture of experimentation: rather than aim to plan and analyse work in detail before doing it, it is preferable to do some of the work, understand the work and then be able to make any forecasts needed. This bias is applied both to the transactional work of the Xanpan team - building software from requirements - and to the adoption of Xanpan and Agile in general.

It is not possible to foresee all the implications or needs of changing the way a team works. Nor is it possible to see the knock-on effects on the wider organisation. Therefore do it and see what happens.

The recipe is:

- Identify a practice, tool, technique, whatever from somewhere else.
- Decide what it would mean to your team: what would you do differently?
- Set a time frame: an iteration, two iterations or maybe more.
- Make the change, and at the end of the period assess whether to keep it or revert back.

It is tempting to suggest teams also decide the criteria by which they wish to judge a change at the same time as deciding how long they will run the experiment. While this might often be a good thing to do, it may lead to unexpected behaviour.

As a possible modification to this experimental process, a team might like to do a trial before embarking on the experiment fully. This could mean one or two team members trying the technique to better understand it first. Or it could mean running a short experiment (one iteration or less) and using the experience to better construct the full experiment.

There are probably some other ways to modify the experiments. Experiment.

8.13 References

Goldratt, E. M., and J. Cox. 1993. *The Goal: A Process of Ongoing Improvement.* Gower Publishing Ltd.

9 Technical Practices

'Quality is Free'. (Crosby 1980)

'The bottom line is that poor-quality software costs more to build and to maintain than high-quality software, and it can also degrade operational performance, increase user error rates, and reduce revenue by decreasing the ability handle customer transactions or attract additional clients'

'For the software industry, not only is quality free as stated by Phil Crosby, but it benefits the entire economic situations of both developers and clients' (Jones, Bonsignour, and Subramanyam 2011).

In this chapter I would like to outline some of the technical practices I believe enhance software quality. I do not intend to describe in any depth any technical practice for improving software quality. Nor do not intend to survey all the possible technical practices available to software teams for improving quality. There are many, many, good books on these subjects, for example (Freeman and Pryce 2009; Feathers 2004; Adzic 2011; Fowler and Beck 1999; K. Beck 2002; Wynne and Hellesor 2012), to name a few. Which books, journals or blogs you consult depends on your technology.

However, and I wish to be unequivocal here:

Unless a team is actively working to improve software quality, not only will Xanpan fail, but any
attempts at Agile are also likely to fail.

Specifically, if a team is not practising test-driven development
as they write code, they are a) probably not Agile, and b) likely
to encounter problems in the near future.

9.1 Test-Driven Development

Test-driven development (TDD), also called 'test first development' and several other names, comes in two distinct flavours.
Probably the most common form, and one which is synonymous
with TDD, is automated unit testing, i.e. developers writing
code to test the code they are about to write themselves. Unless
otherwise specified in this text, like elsewhere, the term TDD is
taken to mean unit test-driven development.

The second is acceptance test-driven development (ATDD), i.e.
acceptance tests specified by a business representative (business
analyst, product manager or other) and frequently implemented
by a professional tester.

Unit test TDD tests very small pieces of code, while ATDD tests
larger bits of functionality such as entire components, modules or
even systems. These two variations on test-driven development
will be discussed individually next.

What unifies both TDD and ATDD is that the tests are specified
before any production code is written. Before thinking about
(designing) how the system will work, tests that will be used to
measure it are put in place.

Underlying the ideas behind TDD, ATDD and many of the other practices described here is the desire to get fast feedback. When a test, or a review, fails, the originator needs to know fast. When this happens they have a fresh memory to help them fix the problem.

Just as important, the problem doesn't advance through the system. So often faults that could have been prevented at the first stage enter the system, and when they are found, create all sorts of problems. I am convinced - although I have never seen a study - that the amount of management time spent on bugs (prioritisation, assessment, scheduling, arguing, etc.) dwarfs the time spent by programmers and testers.

Some years ago I heard Keith Braithwaite point out that in other engineering disciplines engineers use measuring tools to specify and assess their creations. For example, an engineer asked to build a bridge across a river will measure the width of the river, probably in metres or feet. He will assess and specify the load capacity of the bridge, perhaps in kilograms or pounds. He will consider traffic flow, say in cars per hour or people per minute, and so on.

Bridge engineers have a set of standard tools for measuring the things they are about to create, and for assessing whether they have met the standard.

Keith posed the question: *what are the equivalents in software engineering?*

The answer is: the tests.

Because of their originality, software creations lack the uniformity of bridges. (Although as the Millennium, or 'Wobbly', bridge across the Thames demonstrated, even bridge engineers get caught out by original designs once in a while.)

Keith's suggestion was that in writing tests software engineers were creating the tools and instruments they needed to assess their own creations. This is what test-driven development is about.

I would add, from my point of view: TDD is also about specifying an end condition. When tests exist first then developers know they are done when their code passes their tests. As in a *for* or *while* loop, a developer needs a termination test. The unit tests form that end condition, when they pass work is done.

Some would argue, with good reason, that 'test-driven development' is misnamed. It would better be called 'design-driven development' or something similar. While I agree with this argument entirely, TDD is the name we have.

Unit testing is by itself nothing new. Programmers have been unit testing their code for decades. However my generation of programmers, the PC generation, seemed to forget the practice. Automated TDD is a reinvention of unit testing. Combining unit testing with automation and a test-first approach changes a very effective practice into an essential practice.

I believe that by 2020 programmers who do not practise TDD will not be able to find employment.

9.2 Test-Driven Development (Unit Testing)

TDD at this level usually involve coders using tools such as JUnit, NUnit and other members of the xUnit family to write tiny function- or method-level tests for every piece of functionality they write. There are books about TDD unit testing in all modern languages I know of, e.g. (Freeman and Pryce 2009; K. Beck 2002).

Although figures vary vastly - and I know of no formal study - it is not uncommon for there to be between two and four times as much test code as there is production code. Teams commonly talk about 'test coverage' as a means of measuring how much of their production code base is covered by unit tests.

One common reason given for coders not following TDD is a lack of time. While it is true that less production code might be written in the same time when using TDD, there is plenty of anecdotal evidence that coders actually work faster then working test-first. My own justification is: the time for TDD comes from time saved by not using a debugger.

A typical coder will spend between 25% and 75% of their average work time using a debugger tool to find, remove and fix defects in their code. Those who practise TDD effectively typically don't use a debugger at all. Bugs simply surrender.

While many developers 'get' the idea of TDD, they fail initially to appreciate the difference a test-first approach makes. Writing tests before production code rather than after production code challenges the developer to learn and think about design up-front.

The second point many developers initially fail to appreciate is just how fine-grained these tests usually are. A test may be testing just a few lines of production code. Writing fine-grained tests before production code drives design and, in suitable languages, encourages an object-oriented approach.

There have been attempts by academics to prove and quantify the benefits of test-first unit testing. One 2005 study used university students in experimental conditions (Erdogmus and Torchiano 2005). The study concluded that test-first development led to more tests being written than when using a test-last style of coding. While test-first did not clearly result in higher quality, it did reduce the variance in quality, because tests removed or prevented some of the worst problems.

Perhaps surprisingly the study also found that developers who wrote more tests achieved higher productivity overall. That is, the extra time spent in writing tests in the first place paid back in time saved later on.

A more recent industry-based study reported a defect reduction of as much as 91% (Nagappan et al. 2008) and shown below. This study is interesting for a number of reasons. Not only is the study more recent and more conclusive, it also shows a significant reduction in defects, but at the cost of increased time. Personally, were I managing any of these teams, this is a time versus quality trade-off I would take happily.

Team...	IBM drivers	Microsoft Windows	Microsoft MSN	MS Visual Studio
Defect density of comparable team not using TDD	W	X	Y	Z
Defect density of team using TDD	0.61W	0.38X	0.24Y	0.09Z
Increase in time taken because of TDD	15-20%	25-35%	15%	25-20%

However, I tend to doubt the increased time for several reasons. Firstly the report notes that time measurement was subjective, therefore, while it might feel as if the developers are going more slowly, they may actually be going faster. However, as we know, people tend to underestimate time, even retrospectively, therefore it is probable that the figure of increased time should be higher.

Secondly, this time measurement only refers to initial development time after adopting TDD. This means that time may well be saved after initial development in testing or after release in support desk calls. In keeping with Capers Jones' findings, more time spent coding can pay back overall (Jones 2008). Indeed, this research paper notes that reduced maintenance will repay this time. In other words, while coding may take longer, time is saved in testing, fixing, retesting, support bug administration, management time and disruption to schedules. The net result is likely to be shorter schedules.

Also, it is common for developers new to TDD to slow down as they climb the 'learning curve' and do TDD for real. As they become more proficient, they speed up again. Indeed they may even go faster, because they are producing better designs with fewer defects.

On first examination the IBM team seem to be under-performing the Microsoft teams. One needs to remember that IBM has understood the importance of quality in reducing schedules and costs since the early 1970s. Therefore it is entirely possible that the IBM team find fewer defects using TDD simply because they start from a much better position, i.e. there are fewer defects to start with.

In the discussion the researchers note that at the time of the study the IBM team had recently expanded by 50% and that some developers had taken short cuts by not running all the tests. This too could explain the lower defect density statistic. That this team achieved good test results and then fell back to bad habits is a not uncommon story. Despite the fact that IBM knows these lessons, it happens.

Unfortunately, at the time of writing, most programming education still fails to teach TDD. The industry as a whole is faced with a massive re-skilling task. For the next few years companies which can adopt and master TDD can gain significant competitive advantage.

9.3 Acceptance Test-Driven Development (ATDD)

The field of automated acceptance test-driven development is by no means as uniform as unit test TDD. A plethora of tools and approaches are adopted. Perhaps the oldest tool in this field is the 'Fit and Fitnesse' pairing, which allows for table-driven tests. (See http://fitnesse.org/ for both tools and related tools.)

More recently the behaviour-driven development (BDD) approach has lead to tools such as JBehave, Cucumber, RSpec and others. Collectively these approaches go under the name of 'Specification by Example'. (See Wynne and Hellesor 2012; Adzic 2011; Chelimsky 2012; Gartner 2013). Although I have classified BDD as a form of ATDD, it may supersede TDD at the unit test level. If a team can't do unit test level TDD, they are going to have similar problems doing BDD. Teams that master unit testing TDD might advance to BDD; other teams might use the two in combination.

These tools require glue code to enable them to interface with the system under test, either to the whole system or to individual components. Thus coders are often involved with the implementation of such systems. While this may appear to be a limitation, it is in fact an advantage, because it forces developers to keep interface code and 'business logic' code separate. This is generally agreed to be a good practice that is unfortunately too easy to fall out of. These tools keep developers honest. One can think of them as 'sub-surface' tools, because they test just below the user interface (UI).

Software coders may well be involved in setting up ATDD systems, and they may even be involved in writing ATDD tests. In Dan North's original description of BDD, coders and analysts paired at the keyboard, writing tests and code together.

While some user interface-driven tools do exist and are used (e.g. Selenium), they are best avoided if possible. Such tools tend to be slower than the sub-surface and over time can limit the effectiveness of testing. One team I know of used Selenium effectively until the full test suite reached eight hours of run time.

A second draw back to all UI testing tools is that they tend to be fragile. Because interfaces can change in small and subtle ways, test with these tools often break and require effort to restore.

9.4 Refactoring

'Refactoring is a disciplined technique for restructuring an existing body of code, altering its internal structure without changing its external behaviour. Its heart is a series of small behaviour preserving transformations. Each transformation (called a "refactoring") does little, but a sequence of transformations can produce a significant restructuring. Since each refactoring is small, it's less likely to go wrong. The system is also kept fully working after each small refactoring, reducing the chances that a system can get seriously broken during the restructuring.' Martin Fowler, http://refactoring.com/

All code bases age and become more difficult to work with over time. Refactoring aims to keep the code base flexible, or 'agile' if you prefer. Undertaking refactoring involves risk, because it takes a working system and changes it while trying to maintain the external appearance of no change.

When automated TDD is in place there is a safety net under any refactoring; without TDD, refactoring is like a circus high-wire act without a safety net. Not only is TDD a pre-requisite for refactoring, the reverse is also true: refactoring is itself an essential part of TDD.

Because TDD design encourages small-scale, piecemeal design, the overall result is an emergent design and occasions when designs need substantial change. This is not wrong, it is nature at work.

I think of two levels of refactoring. There is *refactoring in the small*. This occurs whenever code is written. Developers write a test, write some code to meet the test and then, before they consider themselves finished, they refactor the code (and possibly the test) to ensure that it has good design properties. It is, in other words, code they are proud of, code they are not embarrassed for others to look at.

Working like this, refactoring is a natural part of development. Refactoring in the small is just an everyday part of a programmer's work. There is no need to call it out or tell anyone they are 'refactoring', one might as well say "I'm washing my hands after toilet breaks today".

Fortunately many of the more common refactorings can be automated, and in the current generation of development tools they can be as simple as highlighting a code block and selecting the right option. Such features only tend to be available for the more modern languages that are either interpreted or include reflection capabilities. Languages such as C and C++ may still require refactoring by hand.

Then there is *refactoring in the large*. This occurs when there is a large part of the system that is not good. This might be a class, or it might be a whole module (however that is defined). There might be tests in place, but more likely than not it is legacy code (Feathers 2004). Here there is a major high-wire act to perform.

Refactoring in the large means taking on this challenge. Hopefully it is not an everyday occurrence; it does need to be called out to the rest of the team, perhaps management, and perhaps special time set aside for the task - see the earlier discussion on *Technical Debt (and tax)*. In such cases the risk is so high that it always makes sense to pair-program the work and to write the new code in a test first manner.

In my experience organisations typically allow too little time for refactoring in the large when there is an existing legacy code base. However, programmers are also guilty in such cases of not doing more *refactoring in the small*. The nature of code is that lots of little changes can make a big difference over time.

9.5 Frequent builds

Hand-in-hand with both TDD and ATDD is the practice of frequent builds. When C and C++ were the dominant programming languages best practice was thought to be an overnight build. Each night a server would build the entire source code base from scratch and programmers would receive a report on anything that failed.

Today, with faster machines and languages such as Java and C#, builds are likely to occur many times a day. Every 15 minutes or so is probably the standard to aim for.

In the 1990s a C++ build would just build the code. Today not only will a Java build build the code, it will run many, if not all, the tests. It is common practice to run the entire test suit - both unit and acceptance tests - as soon as the build is finished.

In dynamic languages and interpreted languages like Ruby, PHP, JavaScript, Python and many others, the concept of complete build is largely redundant. However, with a battery of tests, the same concept can be applied. The code might not need building, but the tests can still be run regularly. The feedback can still be generated.

Today there are many tools available to help with frequent builds.

9.6 Continuous Integration

Accompanying automated tests and frequent builds is the practice of continuous integration. When developing code programmers regularly - continuously - integrate their new code with the existing code base. This practice brings conflicts to attention early and avoids mega-merge activities that inevitably throw up many, many conflicts.

While some Agile teams adhere rigorously to a 'one true branch' strategy and will not branch any code, others are prepared to branch and merge.

Personally I think there is a big difference between a long-lived branch with many changes that spends a long time away from the trunk, and a short-lived branch with very focused changes. I remember projects which would branch at the start, and six months later try to merge back in. 'Merge hell' is too nice a term: such situations should be avoided.

Still, I am happy to see teams branch the code on a feature-by-feature basis - maybe per individual user story or blue card - provided the code is pulled in soon, i.e. within days. Modern repository tools such as Git make this kind of 'micro-branching' far more practical.

Some teams prefer to make use of feature toggles to switch features on and off. New code can be added to a production code base, but left off until it is complete. There are limits to this approach, i.e. big refactorings cannot be switched off, and it is essential that teams remove the toggles before too long.

9.7 Source code control

It goes without saying that the above practices - continuous integration and frequent builds - can only be implemented when teams use source code control. For the vast majority of teams today, source code control is a given. They would no more think of working without source code control than they would of trying to cross a road without looking for moving cars. Yet I still meet teams who have no source code control, or are still wondering if they should adopt the practice. With many free open source tools available for source code control - Subversion, Git, the venerable CVS - there is little reason to go without.

That said, there are some systems - some Pick derivatives for example, and even SAP systems - where getting the 'code' into a state where it can be source code-controlled is problematic. Sometimes, as with SQL and COBOL, these problems can be overcome with sufficient willpower, in other cases the enveloping nature of the development tools may prevent source code control. In these cases organisations should question their continued use of tools that do not support source code control.

9.8 Code Reviews

'Most forms of testing average only about 30% to 35% in defect removal efficiency levels and seldom top 50%. Formal design and code inspections, on the other hand, often top 85% in defect removal efficiency and average about 65%...'

'Formal design and code inspections are the most effective defect removal activities in the history of software and are also very good in terms of defect prevention.' (Jones 2008)

Before TDD appeared code reviews, or inspections, were the most effective known means of preventing and removing defects. Indeed this might still be the case; I am unaware of any studies that have directly compared the two techniques. But there is no reason why both techniques cannot be used together.

The formal code inspections discussed by Jones are one form of code review. Many organisations employ other forms of inspection and review, some heavyweight, some lightweight. (Some have questioned the assumptions about just what it is that makes such reviews effective: for more discussion, see Votta (1993);Votta and Porter (1997)]).

While commending code inspections, Jones points out that it is not just code that benefits from review. Requirements and test documents can also be improved through an inspection process. While of obvious benefit when requirements documents and test specifications are large, the benefits are not so obvious when a requirement is a user story and most of the need is communicated via conversations.

Personally I prefer informal one-to-one personal reviews. Certainly the old style big meetings with coder, reviewer, second reviewer, chair and scribe can be expensive. Whether they are more or less expensive than letting a defect escape is an open question.

When code is reviewed in such large group sessions there tends to be a delay between coding and review - if only because reviews must be convened. As a result they are not timely, i.e. the programmers have moved on to the next thing. The second problem is that these groups tend to sample code rather than review everything. When a review only examines code samples rather than reviewing all code, it might be argued the review is more a review of the programmer than the actual code.

Whatever form code reviews take, the important thing is that they need to happen. They can be made more effective over time, but the first condition must be that they happen. Unfortunately in my experience I find that I am often told that organisations conduct code reviews only to find, when I ask a few more specific questions, that the reviews are often skipped.

Also from personal experience I know that some senior developers use reviews to further their own agenda, and on occasions step over into bullying. One of the reasons I dislike reviews conducted over e-mail (or other electronic tools) is that they are a one-way feedback process: the reviewer reviews but has no means of seeing the reaction on the part of the code's author. This can lead to defensive behaviour in future.

Indeed, many teams base their code review thinking on the assumption that more experienced people should review the work of more junior people. This I find offensive; experienced people should both have their work reviewed and learn from the insights of more junior people. Code written by more senior people will in all likelihood need to be maintained by the more junior people in time, therefore it should be understandable to all.

While much of the benefit from code reviews simply rests on having a second pair of eyes read the code, a second - but very valuable - benefit is knowledge-sharing and learning by the reviewed and the reviewer. Code reviews expose individuals to alternative practices and patterns and allow for discussion about better practices. Again, automated or electronically mediated reviews may hinder such discussion.

The first aim of any team should be to ensure that reviews are happening - and happening without bullying or personal point scoring. The second aim for teams should be to make code reviews more effective.

9.9 Pair programming

Extreme Programming introduced pair programming to the world (K. Beck 2000), although in truth programming in pairs was not the invention of the original XP team (see Coplien and Harrison 2004). When programming in pairs, two programmers sit at the same desk, with one screen and one keyboard. One programs while the other watches, reviews and thinks. The two talk about the code, about the design and about the tests.

Periodically they will swap, the keyboard will move from one to the other. The same two people rarely code together all the time; pairs should swap regularly, perhaps daily, so that individuals do not become tired of one another. In practice this makes regular pairing on small teams difficult.

Some have likened pair programming to airline pilots: one flies while the other observes. It is worth noting that it is usually the senior pilot - the Captain - who observes, while the First Officer does the actual flying. This practice is designed to avoid the junior officer feeling inhibited from questioning the more senior officer's judgement.

Formal pair programming is perhaps more talked about than practised. Many programmers, perhaps three-quarters of all, have an instinctive dislike of the idea of pair programming. Whether it is the thought of someone else seeing their code, or sitting with someone else, or the realisation that pair programming is an intense experience, or simply ego, few programmers are keen on the idea when it is mentioned.

Informal pair programming happens more frequently than is often recognised. One programmer asks another for help, or they talk over a problem over coffee. Programmers often like sharing their problems with others, but can be hesitant to formalise the practice.

While I have heard many programmers comment that their "managers would not like pair programming because it looks like two people are doing one person's job", I have never met a manager who has expressed this sentiment. I have however heard a manager comment, with tongue in cheek, that pair programming would reduce the need for desks and save on office space.

The case for pair programming is two-fold. First there is the quality aspect. Code review is good: pair programming is code-reviewing on steroids. It is instantaneous, it reviews every line, every design decision is open to question. So too are the tests.

As in air travel, in software development mistakes are expensive. Having two people work together can reduce mistakes significantly. (Surgery is another field where the cost of mistakes is high, and again one might find two doctors operating together on one patient.)

Secondly, pair programming is intense. Those who practise it do not answer the phone, they do not engage in instant messaging, they synchronise coffee breaks and toilet breaks - they may continue to talk code at the coffee machine but probably not in the toilets - and typically outsiders tend to interrupt them less often. Steve Freeman once commented "After a morning pair programming I can't even decide what to have for lunch on my own".

The intensity of pair programming means that programmers are highly effective. This does however mean that programmers cannot be expected to work long hours and weekends: they would simply burn out.

Whether the benefits of pair programming make the practice economical is far from clear. One study found a positive economic argument: "In conclusion, the potential of pair programming as a viable alternative to traditional solo programming cannot be dismissed on economic grounds" (Erdogmus and Williams 2003). However, the study authors pointed out that in arriving at their conclusions many assumptions had been made that might not hold in every case.

(Capers Jones, who I normally respect, has recently doubted the effectiveness of pair programming: http://namcookanalytics. com/high-costs-and-negative-value-of-pair-programming/. Without understanding Jones' model in more detail, it is hard to address the argument specifically. However my guy feeling is, on this one, that Jones is wrong.)

The best that can be said about pair programming is that the benefits deserve closer examination. Personally from my experience, I think pair programming is effective. However I also believe one cannot judge the case for or against pair programming until developers and organisations have actually tried it, and tried it seriously for several weeks.

9.10 Static analysis

Static analysis tools seem to have a much higher uptake than either code review or pair programming. Perhaps this is because many static analysis tools are now built into developers' other tools, or because even stand-alone tools are relatively cheap. Or maybe, more cynically, it is because behind every static analysis tool there is a company that is aiming to make money and is therefore marketing and selling the tool - unlike either code review or pair programming.

Static analysis tools reside either in the programmer's work environment or as part of the build system, or maybe in both. They read the source code and analyse it for transgressions. While they are very efficient at finding some types of problem - typically code- and function-level issues - they are poor at identifying design flaws. (Although there are some design heuristics they can apply, and the state of the art is always improving.)

The combination of effectiveness and relative low costs makes static analysis tools an easy decision to justify. Indeed most teams I see today use some tool or other.

9.11 Coding Standards

Coding standard - or a slightly less stringent *coding guidelines* - have been a routine part of software quality advice for decades. Indeed Extreme Programming mandated coding standards as part of the XP process. A team really trying to follow Lean thinking would undoubtedly seize on coding standards as one of the few places where the idea of Lean standardisation can be applied (Liker 2004).

Some teams have coding standards and some do not. While I am generally in favour of coding standards - and again (Jones 2008) argues they are effective at raising code quality - they tend to become the subject of intense debate, resulting in much lost time. The discussion is sometimes described as *Holy Wars.*

One mistake teams make with coding standards is to appoint a fairly junior person to write the coding standards - usually because they do not want a senior person distracted from their work. This approach fails because such a person lacks credibility with others on the team.

The opposite mistake is also made: appointing a senior person to write the standards. In this case they do get distracted from core work, seem to spend a long time coming up with standards, and when they do so often produce standards that need detailed explanation to junior people. I have seen several coding standards written by senior developers that seem to be more an exercise in showing how much the developer knows and how little the rest of the team knows.

Another approach is to take a set of coding standards from the web, say Google's standards, or those from an industry guru. This approach tends to fail because nobody actually spends time reading them.

The underlying problem is that coding standards are often applied in preference to education. Good coding standards are written by very knowledgeable programmers, but often the finer points of the standard are lost on those less knowledgeable or experienced.

Thus mandating coding standards is like mandating knowledge: short of opening the programmers' heads and pouring the coding standards in, the approach will not work. Adopting coding standards should be combined with a process of educating everyone.

My advice, modelled on that in *Safer C* (Hatton 1994), is to start with a coding standard from the web. Convene a meeting; an hour or two should be enough to get going. Allow people at the meeting to propose items from the coding standard. (On a large team people might be limited to the number of proposals they can make at one time.) Then vote on the items:

- Items with unanimous agreement can immediately become mandated coding standards. Code reviews and static analysis tools can be used to ensure these are adhered to.
- Items with broad support might be considered advisable. Code reviews and analysis tools might flag these issues, but they would be allowed.
- There might even be a few items with unanimous disagreement. These should also be noted as not accepted.
- Having created a hierarchy of rules and guidelines, everything else in the standard can now be ignored until the next review of the standard.
- Schedule another coding standards review for two to three months time. During the intervening time, follow the agreed standards and provide training to anyone who requests it.
- Vote again on the mandated items. If anything is no longer unanimous, it can be moved down. Allow advisable items that are now unanimous to move up. In the remaining time allow people to propose new standards or guidelines. In fact it is probably best to allow new items to become advisable only when they have been tried in practice.

Now repeat the process every few months. Keep the standards living. Keep people thinking about them. Encourage experimentation and encourage education. Hopefully anyone who wants to see a new rule added to the standards will spend time educating others in the hope of achieving their support when the vote comes.

9.12 Finally

This is by no means an exhaustive list of techniques for improving code quality, although it might be a list of the more common techniques. Nor is this an in-depth examination of these techniques. There isn't space in this text, nor am I the best person to write about these techniques in each and every technology.

Seek out the best techniques and the best writers for your technology base. Constantly strive to do better. One bug is one bug too many. Put in place the mechanisms for preventing it.

Finally, if you are not doing TDD, the balance of probability is that you are not really doing Agile effectively, let alone Xanpan. But you might be, in which case I hope to hear a well thought out explanation of why your team is one of the few exceptions.

9.13 References

Adzic, G. 2011. *Specification by Example.* Manning Publications.

Beck, K. 2000. *Extreme Programming Explained.* Addison-Wesley.

———. 2002. *Test Driven Development.* Addison-Wesley.

Chelimsky, D. 2012. *The RSpec Book.* Pragmatic Programmers.

Coplien, J. O., and N. B. Harrison. 2004. *Organizational Patterns of Agile Software Development.* Upper Saddle River, NJ: Pearson Prentice Hall.

Crosby, P. B. 1980. *Quality is free: the art of making quality certain.* New American Library.

Erdogmus, H., and M. Torchiano. 2005. "On the Effectiveness of the Test-First Approach to Programming." *IEEE Transactions on software engineering* 31 (1).

Erdogmus, H., and L. Williams. 2003. "The Economics of Software Development by Pair Programmers." *The Engineering Economist* 48 (4).

Feathers, M. 2004. *Working Effectively with Legacy Code.* Prentice Hall.

Fowler, Martin, and Kent Beck. 1999. *Refactoring: improving the design of existing code. The Addison-Wesley object technology series.* Reading, MA: Addison-Wesley.

Freeman, S., and N. Pryce. 2009. *Growing Object-Oriented Software, Guided by Tests.* Additon-Wesley.

Gartner, M. 2013. *ATDD by Example.* Addison-Wesley.

Hatton, L. 1994. *Safer C.* McGraw-Hill.

Jones, C. 2008. *Applied Software Measurement.* McGraw Hill.

Jones, C., B. Bonsignour, and J. Subramanyam. 2011. *The Economics of Software Quality.* Addison-Wesley.

Liker, J. K. 2004. *The Toyota Way.* McGraw Hill.

Nagappan, N., E. M. Maximilien, T. Bhat, and L. Williams. 2008. "Realizing quality improvement through test driven development: results and experiences of four industrial teams." *Empirical Softwae Engineering* 13: 289–302.

Votta, G., Lawrence,. 1993. "Does Every Inspection Need a Meeting?" *ACM SIGSOFT Software Engineering Notes* 18 (5).

Votta, G., Lawrence,, and Adam Porter. 1997. "What Makes Inspections Work?" *IEEE Software* 14 (6).

Wynne, M., and A. Hellesor. 2012. *The Cucumber Book.* Pragmatic Programmers.

10 Planning beyond the Iteration

Notwithstanding unplanned tasks - which might, or might not, be significant - the main planning set piece is the iteration planning meeting, held every two weeks or so. While iteration planning gets all the attention - and a large section to itself in this text - it is not the only planning that happens in Xanpan. There are two more plans that look further ahead. All three plans are recurring cycles, because all three plans are rolling plans: they are regularly updated.

The end of the iteration planning meeting is the moment in time with the greatest certainty over the longest period. At this point the output of the next two weeks is as certain as it will ever be. If a team has a good track record and the numbers to benchmark itself by, there can be near certainty about some of the results.

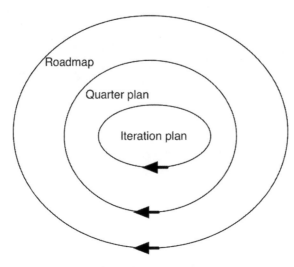

Three planning circles

The other two plans never approach this degree of certainty. People may stamp their feet and demand certainty, even promise not to change their mind, as much as they like, but this does not make it so.

While I think of the three plans as forming concentric circles, they are probably better described as *planning horizons*. The first horizon, the iteration plan, looks two weeks into the future. Of course, if the iteration length is longer or shorter than two weeks, it will have a different horizon. As the iteration proceeds the horizon gets closer; once the end of the two weeks is reached then the plan - the horizon - is reset.

The quarterly plan looks at most 12 weeks into the future, typically six iterations. This is a rolling plan; it is in a constant - perhaps daily - state of flux. When the next iteration starts the first piece of the quarter plan moves to the iteration plan and from 'probable' to 'scheduled'. Next the plan needs extending at the other end. These plans consider both value and effort in the coming quarter.

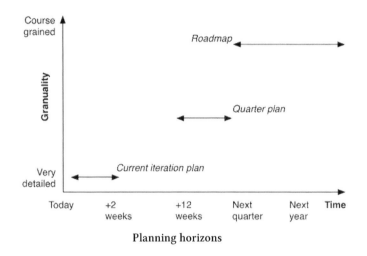

Planning horizons

Further out still is a roadmap. This picks up where the quarter plan finishes, at the end of the next quarter. These look one year, two years, maybe five or even more into the future. They are entirely speculative and focus largely on value; at this range effort estimates are worse than useless because there is so much change.

Many people assume planning to be synonymous with scheduling, putting work in a plan is seen as putting it on a schedule. But in truth scheduling is simply one aspect of planning. Planning is an exercise in looking into the future to learn about what might happen and perhaps prepare for it. In software development this preparation might involve design thinking or requirements investigation to name just two activities.

There is another way of considering the same model, shown in the next diagram. Work that is a long way off is possible, but not certain. As work approaches, it moves from the realms of far-out possible and becomes increasingly certain. Nothing in software development is completely certain until it is delivered and in use. 'Scheduled' is about as close to certain as any planning process can achieve.

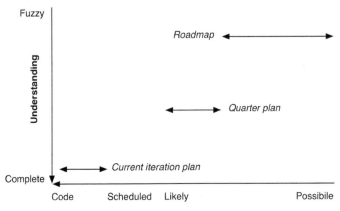

From fuzzy possibility to understood certainty

At the same time as possible work is getting closer in time and certainty, the level of understanding is also increasing. As the understanding - learning - increases the work might be changed, delayed or even cancelled.

Initially ideas on a plan may be highly speculative, little more than possibilities. But once time passes and for off ideas approach implementation they enter the realm of 'scheduled' where there is little space for ambiguity. Once it reaches code level there is absolutely no space for ambiguity: the coding process will wring every ounce of ambiguity from the work. Until quantum computers are perfected, computing will remain a deterministic activity.

10.1 Iteration Planning

Perhaps the reason iteration planning gets all the attention is that it is the most prominent of all the three planning cycles. It is the most regular planning, it is the most collaborative planning, and the plans produced have the highest certainty.

Iteration planning has a chapter to itself that deals with the messy details of the planning session. Right now it is worth saying a few words about the collaborative nature of iteration planning.

Iteration planning in Xanpan is a highly collaborative process, and the planning meeting should involve all team members who will be involved in doing the work. By involving everyone, not only is all expertise brought to bear in planning, but everyone is given a voice and treated fairly.

Some might say that it would be more efficient for a select group to plan while the majority continue to work. However this approach means planning is now a two-stage process: the plans are made, then communicated to the majority.

Leaving aside fairness, leaving aside specialist knowledge, this approach is itself time-consuming. Plans are still made, one or more people then have to communicate the plan, and many people need to listen to the plan. The two-stage process creates space for different understandings. It also reduces the incentive to action.

Planning may take longer when everyone is involved, but action happens sooner.

10.2 Quarterly Plans

Few teams live completely in the moment. At the very least teams are usually surrounded by stakeholders who have an expectation of what will happen next. In my experience someone needs to pay attention to these stakeholder and their expectations. When nobody is paying attention to what comes next, teams hit problems of one sort or another.

Even when a team is overrun with urgent requests, late-breaking urgent bugs and oscillating stakeholders, it helps to have someone take a longer view. Even if the longer view only consists of identifying these forces and communicating back appropriately, someone needs to do it.

There is little point in planning too far ahead: the further in advance plans are made, the more likely they are to change. Without any thought about what comes next, the team could find themselves in the next planning meeting with nothing ready to work on.

While businesses crave flexibility, they also demand predictability, or at least forward thinking. Development does not exist in a bubble, it needs to synchronise and work with other functions. The difficulty is: too much forward planning, too far ahead or in too much detail only increases the likelihood that things will change.

According to Capers Jones (Jones 2008) the industry average for requirements change and growth is 2% per month. Looking a year ahead would mean a 24% change average; add in the effect of compound change and 24% increases to close to 27%. Over two years change will exceed 60% and at 25 months close to 100%

of requirements will have changed. (These calculations exclude the effect of work done. Mortgage-style compound interest rate calculations can be used if the requirements are considered as the principle and deliveries considered as the payments.)

A further danger is that the more detail a plan has, the greater the appearance that the plan represents what will happen. The greater the amount of detail in the plan, the greater the chances that someone will mistake the plan for reality, a prediction of what will come to pass.

In Xanpan the answer to this problem is: a quarter plan. The quarter plan is rolling: it looks 12 weeks or so into the future, it speculates on what might come in the next six iterations. Think of it as six buckets, labelled +1, +2, +3, +4, +5 and +6.

Bucket +1 contains the stories expected in the iteration after this one. Bucket +2 contains the stories that might go into the iteration after that. Bucket +3 the iteration after that, and so on.

Six buckets for six iterations, 12 weeks

Each bucket is filled to approximately the capacity of each iteration, measured by velocity. For example, if a team is currently averaging 15 points an iteration, then bucket +1 might contain stories totalling 16 points, bucket +2 might contain 14 points of stories and +3 18 points worth. (These points are calculated using the *ballpark* estimates discussed in iteration planning.)

Velocity is always changing, teams often reach a stable average but not always. The point of measuring velocity is primarily so the team knows how much work to attempt in the next two weeks, it is a form of work in progress (WIP) limit. This idea can be extended a few weeks into the future with each bucket having an approximate WIP limit. The aim is to smooth flow and pace preparation work.

As a side effect some degree of forward scheduling can occur but the contents of these buckets are in no way promises or commitments. They are possibilities. Granted, the stuff in bucket +1 is far more likely to appear in the next few weeks than the stuff in bucket +6, but that is the nature of life. The further one looks into the future, the greater the uncertainty.

While the programmers might have some awareness of what is in the buckets, they are focused on the coming iteration. Requirements and specification team members (Product Owners, product managers, business analysts, requirements engineers and others) all need to be on hand for questions about the current iteration (and might be involved with the testing), but also need to ensure that the items in the buckets are ready to go when the time arrives.

Since quarterly plans only look a few weeks into the future, using the team's recent velocity is a reasonable benchmark. Velocity on all teams fluctuates, up and down; going too far into the future is unreliable. Secondly, over a 12-week period it is unlikely that team composition will change much, so ballpark estimates are reasonable. Over longer periods existing team members leave, new people join the team and so on.

It is worth repeating the warning from Goodhart's Law: if velocity is used as a target rather than a measure it will loose its efficacy. Rallying a team to reach a higher velocity will induce inflation and destroy what little predictability exists. Schedules made on the basis of velocity are not promises or commitments, they are possibilities.

When the next iteration planning meeting arrives, the work presented for development will largely come from the first bucket, the +1 bucket. Some new items might have appeared recently, so might jump the queue. As a result, some of the items in the +1 bucket might not get included and might be pushed back to a later bucket. Or it might be that items selected from the first bucket might not be included. This could be because when broken down they require more effort then originally envisaged. Or maybe in discussion questions are raised about the nature of the work. Whatever, items might be pushed back.

It is also possible that for various reasons there is capacity in the iteration to take some items not in bucket +1. In which case bucket +2 is quickly brought into play and items selected from there.

As soon as the meeting is over the developers and testers start work on the stories and tasks selected. The requirements specialists now need to roll the plan forward. The now empty +1 bucket moves to the back of the queue. And (at least conceptually) all the buckets are renumbered, so +2 becomes +1, +3 becomes +2 and so on.

With the buckets relabelled they need to be rebalanced. Perhaps the +1 bucket now contains more work than is realistic and something needs to be pushed back to +2, which in turn means something else is pushed back. All the time real-world priorities and needs are shifting, so some items might be pulled forward or pushed back.

The quarter plan will probably be shown to other stakeholders to gain their insights and feedback. As a result the plan will change; plans are a cheap way of exploring how the future might unfold and assessing how to respond.

The key point is: quarterly plans are rolling and changing.

10.3 Release plans

Previously quarterly plans were called 'release plans'. When teams make software releases aligned with iterations (e.g. every two weeks at the end of an iteration), this makes sense. For teams that release less often, say monthly every second iteration, the name 'release plan' becomes a little confusing. It becomes even more confusing when teams make multiple releases during the iteration.

The term 'quarterly plan' both side-steps these problems and reinforces the limit that the plans are both rolling and short term.

10.4 Roadmaps

Roadmaps look further into the future than quarterly plans. At this range team composition is more variable. Future velocity is more variable and the work involved in any potential feature more variable.

Beyond three months effort estimates are best avoided. The emphasis should be on value not effort. If effort numbers are needed then it is more sensible to use the historic average story size in planning rather than ballpark estimates.

Firstly this will save the team time. Many of the stories that are discussed will simply go away, so there is little point in having the team review them. Far more stories will be considered than will actually be implemented: as a rule of thumb one third to half of all possible stories can be expected to drop out.

Secondly, at this range the attempts to estimation effort are little more than guesses and detract from assessing the value of possible work. The granularity of items will be quite large, and many of the details yet to be decided, therefore there is little point in any estimate. However there is a lot of point in determining the real value of potential work and deciding which parts contain the most value.

Too often debates about what should be done become debates about "How long will it take?", with one side saying "It can't take that long!". Unfortunately such debates neglect the value of possible work, let alone the difficulty of producing long-range effort estimates.

In assessing the value of work - a feature or product - the effect of time on value should also be considered. Some features may be highly valuable if released soon or before a certain date, e.g. before Christmas. But the same feature may be worth far less if released later or after some specific date.

On a roadmap product, company, cultural, national and economic rhythms and events should be visible. For example, a company may exhibit at industry trade shows. Most of these shows occur at approximately the same time each year. A roadmap looking years ahead should have the key trade shows marked on it where the company will need to demonstrate new products.

Companies have their own timetable too: venture capitalists typically invest for two to five years. This dictates when the company will be in growth mode, when new products need to be introduced and when costs need to be trimmed.

Customers may have their own rhythms and events which inform the roadmap: Christmas, summer holidays, tax year-end, school years and other events may make some dates better or worse for introducing a new product than others. Legislative changes and other Government activities are also usually visible a year or more in advance. Companies operating internationally may need to consider multiple legal and political contexts.

Then there are less regular events that can also be spotted in advance: the introduction of a new Windows version, new Intel processors and international standards may all be worth including.

All of these events and rhythms should be on a roadmap. In fact, these events can provide the initial framework for the roadmap. So too should technology changes. Details may not be so clear here, but it is still possible to see industry trends - the move towards Service Oriented Architecture, Software As A Service, the rise of Mobile and others are all in progress as I write. Nor is it just the arrival of new technologies. The passing of old technologies needs the same consideration. This is important both for one's own technology base - some clients still have Visual Basic 6 in their production code despite its retirement several years ago - and also for the opportunities it provides.

Take airlines for example: planes don't last forever; individual airlines need to replace their older aeroplanes from time to time. If their last big order was six years ago, and they normally keep planes for 10 years, then there will be an opportunity in a few years. And not just for Boeing and Airbus: new aeroplanes need seats, in-flight entertainment systems, communications networks and much more.

Then there are your own technology challenges and goals. Some of these will be related to industry moves, while others will be of your own making. Thus technologists also need to be part of roadmap creation.

Product roadmaps are also an important means of marrying company strategy with product strategy. A product roadmap will be informed by the strategy the company is pursuing, and the strategy it sees itself pursuing in future. The roadmap will also feed into strategy setting by showing opportunities and possible changes.

Customers you intend to target for more sales, markets you wish to enter, markets you wish to withdraw from, new products and product extensions. All of these and more can be included on a roadmap.

As with quarterly plans, much of the value of the roadmap lies not in the resulting plan but in the creation process itself. As with quarterly plans, roadmaps should be shown and feedback incorporated. Again, roadmaps are rolling and in a constant state of flux. Roadmaps are a learning tool, perhaps even a form of *scenario planning* (Schwartz 1991).

Time passes and the first items on the roadmap will pass onto the quarterly plan and from there to the iteration plan. At the same

time the final date on the roadmap will roll forward and more
items will appear on the other end.

10.5 Too fast for planning?

For teams operating very fast, with short response and delivery
times, the question arises as to whether there is actually any need
for forward planning. For example: suppose a team could deliver
(almost) any request in five working days. Could they dispense
with planning?

Certainly they could reduce their planning horizons on iteration
planning and quarterly plans. Iteration could become weekly,
or dispensed with all together with a 'full Kanban' approach in
which work is pulled as capacity becomes available. Quarterly
plans could shrink accordingly; they might become monthly
plans, looking four iterations ahead. Possibly they could be
dispensed with entirely.

For roadmaps the answer is slightly different. Roadmaps should
align with company strategy where possible - especially for a
small company with few products - to imagine the two becoming
the same thing. The company strategy is the roadmap, and vice
versa. In a larger company with multiple products the roadmap
would in effect become the product strategy that would be
aligned with company strategy.

Let us assume for a minute that a team can operate without any
form of forward planning. Now the question changes from "Does
the team need a forward plan?" to "Does a forward plan add
more value than it costs?"

The cost side of this question is relatively easy to address: the time spent in planning, the resources (e.g. analysts reports, travel expenses) used as part of the planning and so on can be added up. More difficult to quantify are the indirect costs of plans: the mistakes and promises made because someone mistakes the forecast plan for actual future reality.

The value obtained from such a plan is very hard to quantify simply because it is difficult - certainly impossible for me - to value what is unknown. For example, suppose one of your smaller customers is actually the local subsidiary of a global giant, and the whole company is a potential customer?

Obviously, forward planning is not just about technical issues: done well it is about market, customer and product research more than technical.

Finally, planning, particularly at the strategic and roadmap level, is not only about looking forward (Mintzberg 1994). It is also about making sense of the past. Strategy is in part forward-looking - forecasting what might be and putting resources in place - and in part backward-looking, learning from what has happened, finding the commonalities and building on them.

Could a team forsake forward planning altogether? Probably. Should a team forsake forward planning altogether? Probably not.

10.6 Finally

Roadmaps look a long way into the future and are highly speculative. They contain no certainty whatsoever. Quarterly plans look into the medium term, the near future, and while they are by no means certain they describe what is quite likely. Iteration plans look at the immediate future and are the closest thing one will ever get to certainty in software development.

Everything can be thrown off course by unplanned work, but peeking into the future, thinking about what might be and what future priorities are, can help reduce unexpected and unplanned work.

10.7 References

Jones, C. 2008. *Applied Software Measurement.* McGraw Hill.

Mintzberg, H. 1994. *The Rise and Fall of Strategic Planning.* FT Prentice Hall.

Schwartz, P. 1991. *The art of the long view.* New York: Bantam Doubleday Dell.

11 Board 3 - planned, unplanned and improving

The next board is another from a Cornish company. This picture was taken just after the team created the board, before they did any work, so it shows a perfect board at the start!

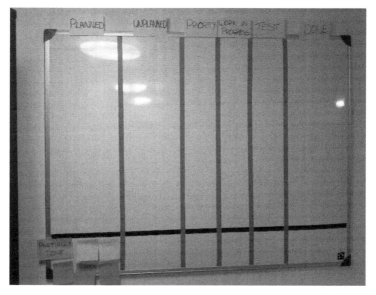

Figure 11.1 - A fresh Xanpan board

As should be obvious by now this board, like the ones seen previously, models the workflow. Visualising the workflow through the board helps teams to reason about the way they work and see problems. I think of Xanpan boards as being like the Pompidou centre in Paris - the plumbing is on the outside, in this case the workflow and work in progress. You can see the stuff that is normally hidden inside. In time changing the board will change the workflow.

11.1 Planned and Unplanned

The problem companies and teams face is that they have both planned and unplanned work to do. Typically this is some project they are working to deliver, but they need to work on support issues - bug fixes - as well. Unplanned work is not confined to support issues, though - sometimes it comes from clients who shout very loud (sometimes called 'decibel management)', or managers who can't say no, or customers who refuse to wait a few days. Indeed, sometimes this would be the wrong thing to do.

The Scrum answer to this is to stamp on the unplanned work. The team is locked - remember commitment and the Sprint-goal? This unplanned work is a problem the Scrum Master should stop - or declare *Abnormal Termination of Sprint*. This isn't a very useful answer, particularly in small companies: the truth is, things are more complicated than that.

The ultimate solution is to look at the reason unplanned items are arising and try to address the root cause. In time it might well be possible to do that, but right now we don't want to block the team's transition, although in the long term this might be the way of the world for such a team.

However it is wrong to automatically view unplanned work as somehow *wrong* or *bad*. True, it may disrupt project work and, by the criteria set down by the project management industry, be seen as problematic, but...

Just because work is unplanned does not mean it is valueless. Unplanned work should be recognised as a potentially valuable activity. Indeed the value of unplanned work should be assessed in the same way as project work. Unfortunately 'business as usual' has become a dirty word in too many companies, *projects good, BAU bad* is the unspoken mantra. Driving unplanned work out of a system may drive out value.

The Kanban answer to unplanned work would be to go in the other direction: run all work as 'unplanned' and just restock the to-do queue as needed. However this robs the team of the rhythmic certainty of iterations. Many of the teams I see need to move away from seat-of-the-pants decision-making and knee-jerk reactions. Adopting regular iterations builds in decision-making points and helps individuals understand their roles.

Xanpan keeps iterations/sprints, but allows for unplanned work. To do this we design a board that begins with the three columns:

- Planned
- Unplanned
- Prioritised (usually this queue is limited)

The next column is usually something like:

- WIP: in development (usually WIP-limited)

The team start as usual: they hold a planning meeting, review blue cards (business requests, user stories) and if necessary break them down to white cards (tasks). These then populate the Planned column. These blues are probably drawn from a traditional product backlog.

At any time work can be added to the Unplanned column. The column is unlimited.

A few minutes before the morning stand-up meeting around the board, someone with authority reviews and populates the Prioritised column. This could be the project manager, business analyst, team leader or someone else: the role and title don't matter; what is important is that this person has the authority to do this. For the team shown in Board 2 this was the joint responsibility of the project manager and business analyst.

This person looks at the work still in the Prioritised queue, and they review the planned work and unplanned work. From these sources they decide on the priorities for the day. When the team gathers they can see what the priorities are. For the sake of simplicity it normally makes sense for the Prioritised queue to be limited and for the priorities to be ordered 1, 2, 3, up to the limit.

If need be priorities can be changed during the day: maybe something even more urgent arrives (or goes away), maybe the prioritised queue empties, or some such. Effort estimates are normally assigned to planned work during the planning meeting. For unplanned work some teams don't bother adding estimates. Individuals could put a quick effort estimate on a card when they actually pick it up. The team shown in Board 1 simply put a retrospective estimate on the card when it was finished. The aim is not to be exact for any one piece of work, but to be generally good enough across multiple pieces of work.

Some might find the idea of not estimating work might strange, but if work is really urgent and cannot wait until the next planning meeting then whether it will have an hour, a day or a week is of little importance. If an estimate is essential the team could quickly do a round of planning poker after the stand-up meeting - although I have never heard of a team doing this and if not limited it could quickly become time consuming.

Importantly, the original source (planned or unplanned) is recorded on the card - maybe a different colour card, maybe a dot, a word, whatever. At the end of the iteration the team can review how much planned and how much unplanned work was undertaken. This can be used for calibration when the team is forecasting.

That is it really: planned, unplanned and prioritised. The first two are effectively queues for the third. Somebody is responsible for balancing priorities.

It is possible that this workflow/board layout is actually a transitional layout. After running with this flow for a while there will be data on how much unplanned versus planned work actually occurs.

11.2 Blocked, dropped

Unlike earlier boards this one has a section at the bottom of each column for work that becomes blocked or is being dropped.

When a card becomes blocked, for any reason, or work is de-scoped, it is moved from the column to the bottom section and a coloured sticky put on the card to indicate why the card is there.

Possible reasons might include:

- Waiting on customer feedback or information
- Customers has decided to drop work
- Waiting on a technical issue (e.g. hardware being pur-chased)
- Waiting on another team member

Several colours are used to indicate what has happened, is hap-pening, to the card. The project manager on the team monitors cards at the bottom of the board and takes action if and when needed. More importantly, this approach also provides data to the team for further improving the flow. Common impediments can be identified, problematic activities called out and so on.

11.3 Improving

This might be the perfect board layout for the team forever. More probably, it can be improved over time - it is an example of Kevlin Henney's Stable Intermediary Forms pattern (Henney 2004).

This is a first cut; the team can, and will, do better. As the team uses this board and learns from it, they will want to improve it. My rules are quite straightforward for Xanpan boards and build on the focusing steps found in the *theory of constraints* (Goldratt and Cox 1993).

Stage 1

1. Model the current workflow on the board: avoid changing it too much to 'how it should be', but you will probably need to modify the workflow a little in order to be able to model it. Make sure you talk through various possibilities for incoming stories and tasks to make sure you have a workflow that will work.
2. Operate the board for at least one iteration (several weeks) and learn from it.
3. Reflect and refine the board: in doing so you will modify the workflow; this should be an improvement.
4. Operate the board some more and start gathering data, qualitative and quantitative, about the flow of work.

This alone might improve your team's performance: you have visibility of the work in progress, you can reason about it, people are better informed, you will make better decisions. But this alone will not solve all your problems. Nor is it the end state: it is just the beginning.

Stage 2

Stage 2 looks at optimising the board and improving performance. To do this, it helps to be clear about what the team want to optimise - what the organisation considers valuable. A lot of organisations and teams want to optimise throughput. Thus the following description assumes that the team also wants to improve the throughput.

Think of the board as a pipeline. There are two ways to improve throughput: make the pipe bigger, or make things move through the pipe faster.

First, seek to move things through the pipe faster:

1. Look at the blocks: why are they blocking or impeding? What can you do about removing them, not just on this occasion, but permanently?
2. Where are the queues building up? Can you rebalance the board, or rather how your people (and possibly other resources) are deployed to even this out?

Continue reviewing the board and looking for improvements forever. But if the time comes when you want a bigger pipe, add people to the team gradually over time. Adding people slows down the existing team - the bigger the team, the smaller the proportional slow down. Growing a team should to be a long-term activity. In fact even teams that have reached a stable size should plan to recruit occasionally, to offset natural losses as people retire or move to new jobs.

Occasionally I see a team attempt very rapid expansion, I call this *foie gras recruitment*, as it is akin to force-feeding the team with new members. Foie gras recruitment is the practice of rapidly expanding - effectively stuffing - a development team with new team members, for example expanding a team of four programmers to eight over a few weeks. This drastically reduces productivity for months while the new team members learn about the system under development and the team finds a new stability.

Stage 3, finally

1. Look at levelling workflow: reduce the peaks and move work to the troughs.
2. Look at increasing the value of the items moving through the pipeline - more and better business analysis and product management.

Those are the rules of thumb. Of course there are exceptions, of course there are other issues, of course they don't cover every eventuality.

I have said little about increasing capacity in this description. Sometimes a bottleneck appears which can be solved by *throwing more resource at it.* If the resource in question is not a person, for example a new server, then it can be quite effective. However, when it comes to expanding capacity by adding more people, it pays to delay for as long as possible. For a start, adding more people is a time-consuming and frequently lengthy process: it is not a quick fix.

Adding more people may make an existing problem worse, may hide it and can make it more difficult to fix. Introducing a change to a team of five is easier than introducing change to a team of 10.

In my experience people - managers specifically - are too ready to reach for more human resources. They would be better denying themselves this option until they have tried other options.

11.4 Board philosophy

Boards model workflow - or rather, boards are the physical visualisation of workflow within the team. In building the first board - their first 'light sabre' - a team needs to decide how much it wants to change the process right now, and how much it wants to defer until members have learned more. Normally teams have at best a vaguely defined process with many ad hoc alterations. Even the simplest boards that don't set out to change process inevitably do.

The general format of the boards is queue, work; queue, work; etc., with a final queue column to catch all the work which is done at the end. At the end of every iteration the final column, the "catch queue", is cleared down and the first queue column repopulated.

That's the general form; there are frequent deviations, as demonstrated by the board in Figure 11.1, which starts with no fewer than three queues. Work columns regularly have work in progress limits imposed on them. As a general rule of thumb I normally start by setting a WIP limit for each column equal to the number of people undertaking work from that column. It doesn't make a lot of sense to have one person try and do two or more things at the same time. Over time, once the board has been in use for a while the WIP limit might go up or down.

WIP limits can, probably should, be broken from time to time. When that happens it is worth examining why. In a stable system with limits that are seldom breached it might be a one off event of little meaning. But when it happens repeatedly it might imply something needs to change. Certainly it might be sign that the WIP limit needs to be higher but before jumping to that conclusion examine the other columns and how the overall system is operating. Repeated breaking of a WIP limit might be a sign that something earlier activity needs changing - or even some later activity.

Most queues are limitless, although again exceptions exist, as in the above. The problem with putting a limit on a queue is:

> What happens when the queue is full? The work needs to queue (in a backlog) somewhere.

When a column is full - i.e. the number of cards is equal to the WIP limit - more work should not be placed in the column. If the preceding column is a queue (usually unlimited), the work can wait there. The fact that a queue column collects a number of cards and keeps getting bigger is itself the sign of an issue that might need to be dealt with. For example, the following work column might need more capacity. This is not simply a case of raising the WIP limit - action needs to be taken to actually increase capacity.

When two work columns, i.e. two columns with WIP limits, are placed consecutively on a board, then when the second column becomes full, work might back up in the previous column. The 'full' state will ripple back across the board. Since some of these cards will be complete but cannot advance, the board will not accurately reflect the state of work.

For example, consider the board in the next diagram:

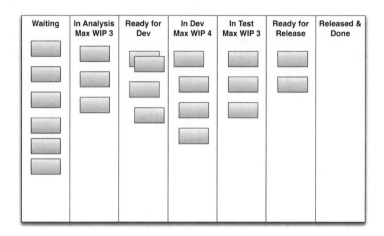

Figure 11.2 - Board to two adjacent work columns

Lots of work is *waiting* in a queue at the start of the board. Three items are *in analysis* and when these are done they will queue in *ready for development.* There is no limit on either of these queues, if lots of work is added to waiting at the start it is probably a sign of unrealistic expectations or an inability to say "No."

If the analysis activity races ahead of development's capacity a queue will form in *ready for development.* This might be a sign that analysis should be slowed or developed expanded. However analysis and development are decoupled, both can proceed at their own pace.

However if development completes more cards than *in test* can accept something has to give. Possibly the WIP limit on the test column is broken to put more cards into the test column. Although sitting in the test column what is actually happening with these cards is unclear. Possibly those responsible for testing are trying to test all the cards in the column, in which case they may be multi-tasking and working inefficiently, consequently cards will leave the column more slowly and further exacerbate the original problem.

Alternatively the extra cards in test might not actually be under test. The test staff may have a mental note of which cards are being worked on and which are not. This is better for overall flow but means the board does not accurately reflect what is being worked on and what is not. Therefore it is difficult to see the actual problem.

Yet another alternative is that the cards are not moved to the *in test* column but held erroneously *in development*. Like in the previous scenario this may interfere with the next task or prevent the board from accurately reflecting the state of play.

Whatever happens, a column with 'too many' cards in it (either a long queue or a broken WIP limit) should cause the team to reflect on what is happening. The board may need changing, WIP limits might need to be raised, but far more often the board is showing a deeper issue that needs to be addressed. Before changing the WIP limit stop and enquire into why the limit needs changing.

11.5 Extending the board

Over time teams may feel they want to extend their boards, either backwards to capture activities that happen before the work hits the team, or forwards to capture activities that happen once work leaves the team. This can be a useful exercise, and understanding the 'before' and 'after' activities can provide useful information.

However, if the team has little or no power to influence these activities, it can be a frustrating exercise. Boards can get bigger, but things may look worse.

Choosing where to begin modelling the workflow, and where to end the modelling, can be hard.

11.6 References

Goldratt, E. M., and J. Cox. 1993. *The Goal: A Process of Ongoing Improvement.* Gower Publishing Ltd.

Henney, K. 2004. "Stable Intermediate Forms" In *9th European Conference on Pattern Languages of Programs (EuroPLoP).* Irsee, Germany: UVK Universitatssverlag Knstanz GmbH. http://www.two-sdg.demon.co.uk/curbralan/papers/europlop/StableIntermediateForms.pdf.

12 Origins of Xanpan

For several years I practised a version of XP (Extreme Programming) that included ideas from Lean. At one point this was described as 'Blue White Red' (Kelly 2007; Kelly 2008). As I moved from practicing to consulting and training, more of the ideas from Scrum permeated, but I have never seen a great deal of difference between Scrum and the process/project side of XP. Or, to put it another way, Scrum, with technical practices from XP (e.g. test-driven development, simple design, etc.) is pretty much XP.

Then David Anderson unveiled Kanban. This pulled the debate back towards Lean; some of the Kanban ideas were already baked into my approach. Kanban caused me to emphasise some ideas and rethink others. For me the big two innovations introduced by Kanban were:

1. Explicit work in progress limits: I had used informal or contextual limits (e.g. the physical size of the board), but making these explicit, actively setting and managing them, I consider an innovation.
2. Multiple columns on the board: I had long referred to the physical board (usually a white board) as the team's 'Kanban board'. Most of these boards simply had *To do, In Progress* and *Done* columns. David's innovation of using multiple columns and queues gave greater detail, more visibility and more control.

Taken together, these two innovations led to far more emphasis on workflow. In effect the workflow was externalised so that it could be seen. I often tell teams that the whiteboard - frequently called *Kanban board* - is a shared *to do list*. Many individuals maintain their own list of things *to do*; for a team, the board is its collective *to do list*.

Technically by exposing the work process and queues Kanban allowed queues to be managed. To the uninitiated this might not seem important but having studied a little queuing theory this opened a whole new dimension of management.

As I followed the Kanban-dev mailing list and reviewed the early drafts of David's Kanban (Anderson 2010) book, two things happened: I incorporated many of the ideas into my own thinking, but perhaps more importantly, I found that the ideas clarified my own thinking and described the way I was working.

Kanban, like the earlier Agile methods, was not so much the product of completely original and brilliant thinking, but captured what was seen to working. Many of the ideas in Kanban, and Agile as a whole, have been floating around, practiced by some, but rarely captured, shared or legitimised. (Not that I wish to detract from the work done by David Anderson in importing Lean ideas to software development, experimenting, capturing and sharing what he and others found.)

At this point my thinking and practise had developed from XP infused with Lean of Blue-White-Red into something with clear traits of Kanban.

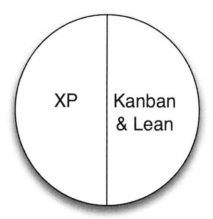

Figure 11.1 - XP with Lean and Kanban

In 2010 I was invited to work on the Grow Cornwall programme. Over the next 18 months I was involved with several Cornish companies, helping them adopt Agile. In truth Agile was a starting point; it was the reason I started working with them. Some of them took to Agile quickly, and as I continued to work with them the real issues the companies faced were less "How should we organise our software development?" and more "What should we build?". It became clear to me that what was needed was a hefty dose of 'the need' side, what was traditionally called 'requirements'.

While I had spent some time working in corporate IT, most of my career prior to becoming a consultant had been spent working for software product companies. This included a stint in Silicon Valley and with one of the more successful UK software vendors (not to mention several less successful ones!). As such I was acutely aware of the differences between 'requirements' inside the corporation and in the product arena, i.e. the market.

This difference can best be summed up by looking at who defines the requirements:

- Inside companies (corporate IT) requirements and speci-fication are usually handled by a business analyst. These people look inside the company to understand the need; development is based on projects that are funded before they start, and users have little or no choice in the software they use.
- Inside software vendors requirements are usually, in suc-cessful companies at least, handled by a product manager. These people look outside the company, into the market, to understand the need. These companies develop products that need to be paid for by customers voting with their own money and choosing one product over another.

I continue to believe this difference is key to explaining the prob-lems many software vendors have. While the product manager role is well-known and utilised in Silicon Valley, it is less well understood elsewhere, particularly in the UK and Europe. (This discussion is explored in more depth in *Business Patterns for Software Developers* (Kelly 2012).)

Sometime in 2011 I started to use the word 'Xanpan' to describe my mix of XP and Kanban, and shortly after I made my first attempts to understand what Xanpan is. It was immediately obvious that product management constituted a third leg to this mix.

Figure 11.2 - Xanpan = XP + Lean and Kanban + Product Management

While product management infuses Xanpan, this does not mean that it cannot be applied inside a corporation: it can. The infection isn't so great as to overwhelm the method; at this level business analysis thinking lies parallel to product management. Indeed, as IT becomes more pervasive inside the corporation and more of the corporation's products include more outward-facing IT aspects, there is a need for business analysts to look outside the corporation.

By now I was mentioning Xanpan in my blog and using the word with clients. Again and again I came across instances where people were adding elements of Kanban to Scrum or XP. Essentially they realised that strict adherence to the 'story must fit in a sprint' rule created problems. In particular, forbidding stories from spanning sprints disrupts flow. This in turn leads to peaks and troughs in different activities during the sprint, especially testing. Those versed in Lean know that levelling such peaks and troughs is necessary to improve production.

Some teams were simply relaxed about sprint-spanning stories, other teams used the idea of 'split stories', and some were, like me, using tasks. And many teams were trying to abide by the 'story completes within a sprint' rule and finding that it caused problems. In one case the team ended up with lots of really small stories, few of which had business value by themselves.

The motivation for allowing stories to span iteration is not to allow for bigger stories or to remove the need to create small stories, rather it is to improve flow and bring business benefit to the fore. Stories should be as small as possible and no smaller.

All this encouraged me to think about the nature of Xanpan: *how was I really advising teams? Where was my advice different to Scrum, XP, Kanban and others? What else was I saying? And what were my underlying principles?*.

I came to realise that I was adding a bunch of 'other stuff' to my prescription which I couldn't really pin down to one source. Much of it came from my studies of modern management, organisational learning and various researches. Hence, in the latest incarnation of Xanpan I imagine it as a more complex mix: XP and Scrum, Lean and Kanban, product management (and business analysis), and some other ideas.

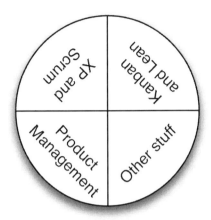

Figure 11.3 - Xanpan mixes lots of ideas

Finally, Xanpan is an approach for developing software. Unlike Scrum, I don't claim it can be used for anything else. I'd like to think it can, but right now I have no stories to tell (yet). Unlike Kanban, I don't claim it is a change methodology - yes it will create change, some directly, some indirectly, but change itself - well, things are more complicated than that.

Right now Xanpan is an approach for developing software and not a lot more. The text in you hands is a description of software development. Maybe one day I will have experience applying of Xanpan elsewhere and I can write about that in another text. Although once one applies Agile outside any form of software development, it looks a lot more like Lean. If you take Xanpan outside of software development the XP technical practices will be dropped - although domain-specific quality practices may be added - at which point Xanpan may well look a lot more like Kanban.

So maybe Xanpan is just an implementation of Kanban within a software development environment. One might say that Kanban is a model upon which Xanpan is built.

In *Changing Software Development* I argued that software developers are in many ways the prototype for future knowledge workers. Software developers have historically had early access to many of the tools that are standard for knowledge workers, e.g. e-mail, web repositories (and Wikis in particular), instant messaging applications and more. As a result software developers have pioneered many of the techniques now considered standard for knowledge work.

Perhaps this trend will continue. Already there are stories of legal and marketing groups adopting Agile-like practices. And as Agile attracts a wider base outside software development, the more those adoptions look like Lean.

Finally, to avoid any misunderstanding... Xanpan is pronounced 'Zan-pan' (like xylophone) and spelled with a capital X, because it is a name!

12.1 References

Anderson, D. 2010. *Kanban.* Blue Hole Press.

Kelly, A. 2007. "Blue White Red - an example agile process." *ACCU Overload* (81).

———. 2008. *Changing Software Development: Learning to Become Agile.* John Wiley & Sons.

———. 2012. *Business Patterns for Software Developers.* Chichester: John Wiley & Sons.

Appendix: Quality

Advocating software quality demands that I define what I mean by software quality. However this is not as easy as it might seem - in fact it is far easier to find fault with definitions of quality than it is to define quality itself.

One reoccurring definition of quality is 'conformance to specification'. Applying this definition in software development presents several challenges:

- Rightly or wrongly, much software is developed without a specification.
- Specifications can be the source of quality problems themselves. Conformance to a poor specification results in poor software. Capers Jones has written "defects in requirements and specifications outnumber coding defects and cannot easily be found by testing" (Jones 2008).
- Software changes during development and afterwards; creating the software often shows up deficiencies and inaccuracies in the specification itself.
- Specifications are often vague. Formal specifications - using predicate calculus and similar - can remove much vagueness, but are expensive and time-consuming to write.
- While specification and code are being developed, the requirements placed on the software change; the final system might conform to the specification but be delivered so late that the specification is out of date.

Software guru Jerry Weinberg has written:

> 'Quality is relative; quality is value to some person.
> Value is what people are willing to pay to have their
> requirements met' (Weinberg 1992).

Weinberg's definition continues the tradition of quality guru Edwards W Deming, who believed that the customer's definition of quality was the only one that mattered. Both are useful definitions, but put the responsibility for defining quality attributes onto someone else's shoulders.

In Deming's case it was the customer who decided value. But as there is seldom one and only one customer for software, it makes more sense to talk about *stakeholders*. This in turn highlights the importance of understanding who the stakeholders are and what they value. This also implies that there may be no common quality attributes that are universal.

Preceding both Deming and Weinberg, Joseph Juran suggested quality is 'fitness for intended use'. For our purposes this definition is of more immediate use. There are some properties of software that I believe are universal and should be maintained to a high standard. These properties are:

- A low number of defects (which means we need to define 'defect', but let's hold that thought for the moment).
- A high degree of changeability, which might also be called *maintainability*, and specifically the ability to expand the system and fix defects.

In the rest of this appendix I argue that, while quality for your customers may be more than these, these two qualities are universal.

Internal and External quality

It is worth at this point differentiating between *external quality* and *internal quality*. For many - perhaps most - products and services, there is little need to differentiate between internal and external quality: everything is customer-visible. If a Starbuck's coffee isn't up to quality standards the customer will taste the difference; if the innards of a television don't work well, the customer will notice an erratic picture.

For software the customer - user - cannot see the internal attributes:

- *External quality* is what customers and users see: they are likely to rate quality on characterises such as ease of use, intuitiveness, the degree to which the software helps them do what they need to do, and how often it crashes or causes them problems.
- *Internal quality*, on the other hand, isn't seen by the users, it is only seen by the technical team. Internal quality concerns attributes about the code, the ease of changing the code, the ease of following the code and the difficulty of enhancing the application.

One analogy might be a car: there are external qualities a customer will see, for example leather upholstery, sleek styling and rapid acceleration. Then there are internal qualities a customer won't see - unless they look for them - the engine, which might be inefficient, slow to respond and emit lots of gasses. But, even here, if the customer chooses to look they can find this out, and over time they will come to notice that the car performs poorly. With software things are much more difficult to distinguish.

It is possible to imagine a product with high external quality but low internal quality, but I have never encountered such an application. While I accept such an application may exist, I tend towards the view that a rotten inside is unlikely to produce a beautiful outside.

Software quality

Quality - both in general and in software terms - has many dimensions, and rather than attempt to define quality as an absolute, it is better to discuss - as would Tom Gilb - qualities (Gilb 2005). While Tom says "qualities" I prefer to say "attributes" as in "What are the attributes of quality wanted from the software?"

Each one of us could - and perhaps should - make a list of the qualities we believe high-quality software should exhibit. For some these qualities would include speed of execution, performance; for others security would be high up the list. Some might nominate the cost of the software, while others would see cost as a non-quality attribute. Let me suggest that everyone would include 'No bugs!' in their list.

These qualities can then be used to measure the software. Is it fast enough? Is it easy enough to use? Does the code exhibit high levels of coupling or high cyclomatic complexity? Indeed

Tom Gilb would suggest it is these qualities, and the level of the qualities rather than functionality, which are the most important aspects of a software product.

While our individual preference could form the basis for an interesting discussion, a more useful perspective would be the properties a development team would define for their product. More illuminating still would be the properties the customers would define for the product. Indeed defining 'what is quality' is an exercise every team should engage in with their customer representatives.

The qualities that make one piece of software 'high quality' might not be the same properties that make another piece of software 'high quality'.

Quality Onion

I have come to believe that software quality is akin to an onion: the many qualities which we desire of software constitute successive layers, each layer wrapping the previous ones. Different individuals, different teams, different products, will have different layers to their onions, and the same layers may appear in different places.

At the core of the onion are two invariable qualities that are true of all software:

- Defects: there is an inverse relationship between the number of defects, and their severity, in a piece of software and the perceived quality of the software. The more defects a piece of software possesses, the lower its quality.

- Maintainability: the more maintainable, changeable, specifically expandable, the software, the higher its quality.

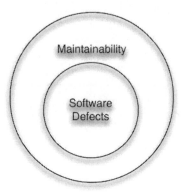

The core qualities of software

Using this metaphor, external quality relates to the outer layers of the onion, those that are seen by the customer in the vegetable shop. Internal quality relates to the centre and inner layers of the onion.

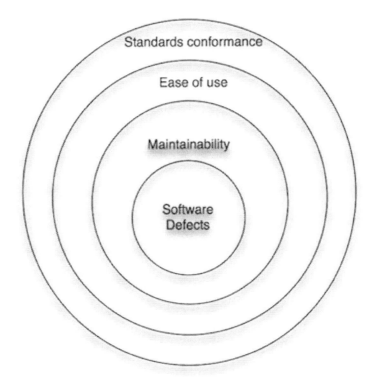

Example of an expanded quality onion

Teams are encouraged to draw their own *quality onions* to decide what qualities are important for their product and to state the relative priority of these qualities. Ideally teams would go further, and not only specify what qualities they expect of the software and their relative priorities, but:

- How they intend to measure each quality.
- The level of performance their customer desires and they intend to aim for.

- What their current performance level is.

Such an approach should be recognisable to students of Tom Gilb.

Defects

Some software defects - colloquially called *bugs* - are objective defects: a calculator that returns 5 when asked to add 2 and 2, or a word processor that causes a machine to reboot. Few would argue that such behaviour was anything other than a defect. However, such objective defects are in the minority. More defects of my experience are subjective: *one man's bug is another man's feature.*

For example, I once worked at an Internet TV company. One software release introduced unexpected behaviour into the programme-scheduling interface. A large UK television company logged a defect report that was duly accepted and entered into the defect list with a high priority.

Several months later the software development team released a software update that fixed the defect. Within minutes the same TV company was on the telephone asking why the scheduling interface has changed. During the intervening months the TV staff had not only worked around the defect, but had actually found this advantageous and changed their working practices to exploit the 'defect'. Unfortunately nobody at the software company had picked this up.

Some companies actually - and usually unintentionally - encourage staff to report defects rather than raise feature or change requests. For example, some software is supplied under a warranty; if the software contains a defect, the supplier will fix it free of charge. But a change request is a billable item. Thus if the customer wants the software to perform differently, it is to the customer's advantage to have the issue accepted as a defect.

A related but subtly different problem exists around accounting standards:

- Developing new software is usually treated by accountants as capital expenditure, 'CapEx'. So spending on software creates a company asset on the balance sheet that is later depreciated.
- Fixing existing software is sometimes treated as an operational expenditure, 'OpEx'. This expenditure does not create an asset, only a debit.

Companies may lay down quotas of CapEx and OpEx in annual budgets. This may encourage staff to log issues as defects, to use up the OpEx budget even if it could be considered an enhancement, or as a CapEx when OpEx budgets are constrained.

In a further twist, some companies will pay staff or contractors different rates for bug fixes as opposed to new feature work. An issue considered a defect might cost less to fix because cheaper coders are used. However, since cheaper coders tend to be less experienced, they may take longer to resolve the issue, negating any saving.

In short, defects can be very subjective.

For these reasons I find it useful to distinguish two types of defect:

- Absolute defects: software behaviour which, according to an objective standard, is considered defective.
- Common defects: any software behaviour which some person is so concerned about that they raise a defect report.

This distinction is useful in discussing defects, but less so in practice. Too many discussions about defects seem to revolve around one side trying to have the other side accept that the defect is or is not absolute.

While morally one might only wish to accept absolute defects, in practice it is better to accept all common defects. If someone considers it worth raising a defect report, then it has some value to them and should be prioritised against other work - defect and non-defect - in scheduling time.

In general:

- All defects need to be administered; some need to be fixed, but all cost time and money to administer.
- All defects cost time and usually money: logging a defect in a tracking system takes time and money in commercial environments. Even if nothing more happens, money has been spent to raise the defect.

  (A defect which results in a call to a support desk may actually result in many calls to the support desk from many different individuals. Associated costs rapidly increase.)

Assuming some action is taken as a result of the log - whether that be a review and 'do not fix' mandate, or an actual fix - more money is expended. Defects that receive a full fix and test are the most expensive.

- Absolute defects, and some common defects, also cost money in terms of system performance, e.g. inaccurate payments from banking systems, lost customers from a online retailer.
- Software with a large number of defect, of any type, recorded should not be considered high quality. High-quality software has few current defects recorded against it, and in all likelihood, few historical defects logged against it.

Changeability (Maintainability)

'A hallmark - if not the hallmark - of good object oriented design is that you can modify and extend a system by adding code rather than hacking it... In short, change is additive, not invasive. Additive change is potentially easier, more localised, less error-prone, and ultimately more maintainable than invasive change.' John Vlissides (Vlissides 1998)

I'm prepared to generalise this to all software, not just OO software. I might even go as far as focusing on the 'rather than hacking it' - although one then needs to define 'hacking'. Good software needs to allow for change rather than having change forced into it.

Actually this quote also provides the attributes we need to define *easy to change*:

- Change is localised.
- Change is less error-prone - perhaps better stated as 'change does not inject new defects'. Bad fix injection has been put at 7% of defect fixes (Jones 2008).
- Change is more maintainable, i.e. changing software does not detract from the changeability of the software.

Whether one says 'ease of change', 'maintainability' or 'changeability', the attribute we are concerned with is the ease with which a program can be changed. After all, software is supposed to be *soft*.

Whether the change be a defect fix, a change to enhance functionality (or remove functionality), improve performance, or any other type of, well, change. Changeability matters more than might be realised. Successful software lives, it changes, it moves on. Unsuccessful software doesn't need to change, because nobody uses it: it is dead.

With changeability comes the ability to retrofit any attribute (quality) that is needed at a later date. Some examples include:

- If it becomes important for the software to work faster, then changeable software can be changed (optimised) to work faster.
- If an application is difficult for users to operate, then changeable software can be changed to present a more user-friendly interface.

- If a defect is found in an application that is changeable, then the defect can be fixed.

Software that is difficult to change might still be changeable to meet these new requirements, but the time and cost of doing so may be prohibitive. Perhaps more importantly, programmer intuition is that programs that are more difficult to change contain more defects. To quote Professor Tony Hoare:

> "There are two ways of constructing a software design: one way is to make it so simple that there are obviously no deficiencies, and the other way is to make it so complicated that there are no obvious deficiencies. The first method is far more difficult."
> C A R Hoare, 1980 Turing Award Lecture.

It is important to realise that maintenance and change of software does not begin at some arbitrary date when the product or project is declared 'done'. Rather, it begins almost as soon as the first line has been written. If a defect is found or a requirement changed after any code is written, then the rework of that code requires changeability. Any development effort that trades off the ability to change against time is potentially short-changing itself, because the some additional effort will need to change work it has already done.

Over the years computer scientists have developed concepts and a few metrics that can be used to reason about software quality. It is generally agreed that good code:

- Has low coupling, i.e. software units limit the extent to which they reference other units, to limit knock-on effects of defects and changes.
- Has high cohesion, i.e. within the construction units there is grouping of similar logic.
- Has well-defined interfaces.
- Has a low cyclomatic complexity: this is one (sometimes contested) measure of how difficult the code is to follow.

Doubtless this list could be extended. The key thing to understand is that we have tools, sometimes imperfect, for assessing and reasoning about code quality.

Recently the Agile and software craftsmanship movements have added another:

- Is tested, i.e. code has been tested, and, as described elsewhere in Xanpan, 'tested' usually means some form of automated tests.

Keith Braithwaite has suggested that in creating tests we create the tools with which to measure software. Other engineering disciplines have common measurement units (metres, kilograms, volts) and tools to measure the units. In software the measurement units may be as unique as the software, and we must craft special measurement tools.

These are the same characteristics Vlissides was speaking about. They are not concepts dreamed up by idealist academics intent on frustrating and confusing the real-world work. There is a reason why such concepts appear again and again in the literature:

they matter, they help keep software 'soft', and they make the economics of software work.

Obtaining the qualities (design)

How you go about obtaining the core qualities, and any other qualities you desire, is entirely up to you. My purpose so far has been to define quality, not to specify how to achieve it.

Broadly speaking there are two schools of though about how to achieve software quality:

- Traditional, 'big up front design' (BUFD) or 'waterfall'

  Through detailed understanding of what is needed, and conscientious software design and architecture, robust software with few defects and high maintainability can be produced. In order to undertake this, a chunk of time is needed before any work begins. The bigger the system is, the longer this time is likely to be, but really there is no way of knowing how much time is needed. Weeks are more common than days, and months more common still.

  This school of thought may also be associated with studious test cycles intended to thoroughly test the software and allow defects to be removed. These test cycles would be better term "Test-Fix-Retest" or "Rework" cycles because usually the time is spent fixing defects which are found.

- Emergent, 'rough up-front design' (RUFD) or "Agile"

  Design activities are focused on the near term, and
  little (if any) attempt is made to architect for more
  than is currently known. This school believes that
  any design will need to be changed in the near
  future, so anything produced should be maintainable, but no more. Since the future is uncertain, any
  speculative design could be wrong, and could result
  in over-engineering, which takes time immediately
  and may actually hinder future maintainability.

  Emergent designers use testing itself as a design
  tool and safety net. The tests 'pull the design', and
  the safety net allows all choices to be changed with
  minimal risk.

One might also ague that there is a third school of thought that
believes quantity is the key quality. This school of thought main-
tains that more software, built and delivered faster, constitutes
quality all of its own. This school rejects - or de-prioritises - the
idea that defects reduce quality, or that maintainability enhances
quality. Members of this school believe that getting something in
users' hands is the key quality.

While recognising that traditional ('big up front design') may,
by some, be considered an option, I reject it. Xanpan embraces
emergent design. Engineers are mandated to make their code
maintainable without over-engineering and complex designs.
This is easier to say, and imagine, than it is to practice. Some

designs will, in retrospect, prove to be over-engineered, and others to be under-engineered.

Xanpan emergent design embraces several design principles from Extreme Programming and Jon Reffries:

- 'You aren't gonna need it', or 'YAGNI': don't over-engineer the solution or create designs to serve some need which is imagined but not requested or known.
- 'Do the simplest thing that could possibly work', rather than using a more complex design, and be prepared to revisit the design later if need be.
- 'Always implement things when you actually need them, never when you just foresee that you need them'.

Of course this creates a conflict. Much of this appendix and book has argued that high quality benefits customers and engineers. This advice might be seen to contradict that argument. This conflict lies at the heart of much engineering:

> How does 'done' create a good solution without going too far?

There is no textbook answer, no fixed set of rules or flow chart that can answer this question. It comes from one's own engineering experience, knowledge, intuition and judgement calls. Sometimes these judgement calls are wrong.

Xanpan recognises that sometimes we 'get it wrong' or 'called the future incorrectly' and we need to revisit designs. In software engineering this is often called *refactoring* (Fowler and Scott 2000).

In practice this means that, rather than taking a chunk of time at the start of a project and doing 'design', then working to that design for the next 11 months, the time is spread out over the whole project. On day one a few hours are taken to design for the next two weeks. During the next two weeks, if some design issue arises, then time is taken to address it. This time is measured in minutes and hours, not days.

Two weeks later a little time is taken to design just enough for the coming two weeks, and the work that will be done. Design is always interactive; it is about getting individuals doing the work to contribute to and agree the solution. It is about creating a shared mental model of how the software hangs together.

Over 12 months the amount of time might be more or less than doing it all up front; that is not the issue. The key point is that design is pulled as needed. If more design is needed, then more design is done.

It is impossible to know in advance how much design is the right amount, how much is too much and how much is too little. In truth we can't measure the quantity of design - the number of UML diagrams and hours spent are but proxy measurement of what is done. Since there is no way of knowing how much is right, how much is too much and how much too little, the approach is to do it as needed.

This approach also sidesteps the question of when design ends and code begins: coding *is* designing. It also means the team needs to be clear on understanding what it is trying to achieve, the qualities and the quality.

Quality and business value

Working from Deming and Weinberg's definitions of quality, 'higher quality' implies 'higher value'. Juran's quality as 'fitness for intended use' holds the same implication only in reverse: a product that is not fit for its intended use cannot recognise the value to be gained from the intended use. (The product might have some other use which delivers value, but that would require a redefinition of its intended use. Once the intended use is changed the product will deliver value, albeit different value from what was originally intended.)

Given that, let me make another statement I believe is true:

> Quality results in business benefit - money made, happier customers, business aims realised, money saved (development costs, support costs, revenue lost, etc.).

Once we accept this, statements like 'quality is free', 'high quality saves money' and 'quality sells' become axiomatic. The aim of 'high quality' is to produce one of these business benefits.

Consequently statements like "We can't afford this much quality" and beliefs like "Lower quality is acceptable to customers, is faster and saves money" are the result of a mismatch in different individual's understanding of what quality is.

For example, one person might believe that customers are happy with buggy software as long as it is available soon, while another believes that customers want bug-free software later. When such mismatches occur, using the word 'quality' is itself a problem, because it means different things to the different parties.

While this relationship between business value and quality might appear circular, it is a consequence of using the definitions above. Starting with a different definition of quality probably results in different logic. I leave it as an exercise to the reader to define their own meaning of 'quality' and derive the argument.

Finally

Returning to Juran's definition of quality as 'fitness for intended use', this is the underlying principle of quality in Xanpan:

1. No product with a significant number of defects is likely to be fit for its intended use. Studies indicate that software with a high number of defects costs more to develop and maintain, and takes longer to do so, than software with low defect rates (Jones 2008).

2. Successful software products have longevity - they last. Therefore software that we intend to be successful needs to be extendable - it needs to live, and for that it needs to be changeable, if only to allow defects to be rectified.

Consequently, for any piece of software engineers need to strive to keep the defect count low and maintainability high. There will be other quality attributes that software products will need, but these will depend on its intended use, its stakeholders, and most of all, those stakeholders we call 'customers'.

While I am prepared to admit there may exist a piece of 'use once and throw away' software for which property #2 may be suspended, I have never encountered such software. I have however encountered pieces of software for which some stakeholder claims "This will be used once and thrown away". In my experience when #2 is relaxed, #1 is also relaxed (intentionally or not). When #1 is relaxed the software never makes it to one use, let alone two, and because #2 was relaxed it is time-consuming, expensive and possibly impractical to fix the defects.

While I have argued for keeping quality high - and Xanpan mandates this approach - this is not an excuse to over-engineer, over-design and gold-plate products.

References

Fowler, Martin, and Kendall Scott. 2000. *UML distilled: a brief guide to the standard object modeling language. Object technology series.* 2nd ed.. Reading, Mass.: Addison Wesley.

Gilb, T. 2005. *Competitive Engineering.* Butterworth-Heinemann.

Jones, C. 2008. *Applied Software Measurement.* McGraw Hill.

Vlissides, J. 1998. "Pattern Hatching: Subject-Oriented Design." *C++ Report* (February 1998). http://citeseerx.ist.psu.edu/viewdoc/download?doi=10.1.1.153.4111&rep=rep1&type=pdf.

Weinberg, G. M. 1992. *Quality Software Management: Systems Thinking.* Dorset House.

Acknowledgements

Some of the articles in this book have been published elsewhere and have been reviewed by others in different contexts. It would be impossible to keep track of everyone whose comments have influenced my writing, but I can at least name a few of them.

The editors and editorial team of ACCU Overload, for reviewing, commenting and even publishing many articles over the years. Most of the articles concerned were published during Ric Parkin's time as editor, although John Merrells and Alan Griffiths also deserve thanks for their time editing Overload before Ric.

Ed Sykes, Paul Grenyer, Giovanni Asproni and other ACCU members have all at times reviewed and contributed to my work. Conversations with these and other ACCU members have been fundamental in shaping my view of the software development world.

Xanpan, both as an idea and a manuscript, has benefitted from comments and encouragement from Jon Jagger, Dom Davis, Sunish Chabba, Giovanni Asproni, Seb Rose and Schalk Cronje in particular. Thank you! With the release of this manuscript to a wider audience I hope to add to this list in future revisions.

Particular thanks are owed to Lindsey Brodie for reviewing my 'Requirements 10 Step' the model. Implicitly thanks are due to Tom Gilb for several of the ideas embedded in this model. While Tom might not agree with every aspect of the model, his ideas underlie much of the thinking. Indeed Tom has been a great influence on all my thinking, perhaps more he will ever recognise! (The '10 Step model' is not included here, a new requirements model but will be added later.)

As I said in the introduction, many of the ideas in Xanpan have been 'discovered' and practiced independently of myself. That others reach the same position serves to validate the idea. In particular I'd like to thank Rachel Davies and Arber Pilana for discussing the similarities and differences of their team.

I also need to thank the unwitting guinea pigs and early adopters of some of these ideas - some will recognise themselves in the text! At the risk of offending anyone at missing out a name, I would like to maintain an element of client confidentiality. (This also means I can share some of the downsides!)

Thanks too to Nicki Kelly and Steve Rickaby of WordMongers for help with editing and production. Last, but not least, to Taissia Chinina for her patience and support.

Version History and coupons

- Version 1.0, 1 August 2013: First publication to general public
- Version 1.0.4, 15 September 2013: Added quality appendix and discussion of quality in principles
- Version 1.1.0, February 2014: Full copy edit plus other updates (version unpublished)
- Version 1.1.1, 2 March 2014: New cover page and A5 layout
- Version 1.1.2, 10 April 2014: Emergency fix, several chapters missing from 1.1.1
- Version 1.1.4, 26 April 2014: Minor changes in preparation for hardcopy version

In keeping with LeanPub practices this book will be updated, corrected and expanded over the months which follow. Sometimes these will be small increments, sometimes big ones.

Some versions of this book are being made available with coupons for free or discounted related books. The coupons, if any, will be included on the subsequent - final - pages.

Coupons for paperback buyers

Buyers of the physical paperback version of this book may also download the e-book version for free.

Visit https://leanpub.com/xanpan and use the coupon codes:

- **PaperbackBuyer2014** - valid during 2014
- **PaperbackBuyer2015** - valid during 2015

These coupons will entitle the user to a free download and updates in PDF, mobi or epub format.